Mat Dry

THIS
is Africa
True Tales of a Safari Guide

ISBN: 1466485736
ISBN 13: 9781466485730

To Hope and George,
my two greatest inspirations

INTRODUCTION

" *You follow your heart, Mat,*" Barry says in his thick Afrikaans accent, pointing at my chest. At 6'3" and two hundred and fifty pounds, Barry towers over me. He looks like a man who could tackle the wilds of Africa, and so he does. Barry is a *safari guide*. Who knew there was such a thing?

We stand in a bar on the banks of the Chobe River, Botswana. I am nineteen days into my overlanding trip from Cape Town, South Africa, to Livingstone, Zambia. I am already in love with Africa and trying to figure out how I can return to Africa for good after my vacation is over.

"I've been doing this for seven years now, Mat. I used to be very unhappy working as an engineer. I went to school to be a safari guide and, here I am, loving every minute of every day." Who knew there were schools where one could learn how to become a safari guide?

For two hours I have bombarded Barry with questions about his life in the wilds of Africa. "Have you seen one of these? Have you ever run into one of those? Have you ever had to do something when you encountered that creature?" Barry answers every one of my questions with an enthusiasm that matches my own. And he has stories. Lots of stories.

"I can see you're interested in this, Mat. From what I can tell, this job would be perfect for you. You would be perfect for this job. Let me tell you something that happened to me and my clients not too long ago…

"I was asleep in the Okavango Delta. We had set up our four tents to form a square in the middle of the campsite. Sometime around midnight, I woke up to this terrible roaring, screaming, and chattering, right in the campsite. It was terrifying! I jumped up to pull on my pants. Something unbelievably powerful bowled me over, knocking the breath out of me. As soon as I caught my breath, I yelled, 'Stay in your f–king tents!'

"I heard a ferocious digging and scraping along with my clients' screaming from the tent directly outside my door. I unzipped it and looked out to see what the hell was going on. Sure enough, a huge male lion is attacking a honey badger who is trying to bury himself backward under that tent. You know how ferocious badgers are, right? Well, every time the lion moves in for the kill, the badger gets him with a claw or bite, and the lion goes crazy. When the frontal attack doesn't work, the lion tries to get the badger from above and ends up *on* the tent and my people.

"So, I'm screaming, they're screaming, the honey badger is screaming, the lion is roaring. It is total chaos! Then, just as quickly as it appeared, the honey badger made a break for it into the darkness with the lion in pursuit. Gone as quickly as they came. Heh, heh! It was wonderful…" He lets that sink in.

"You could be experiencing that every day of your life, Mat." That's when he points at my chest. "*You follow your heart…*"

So I did. In 2006, at thirty-five, I quit my job as a director of a tennis club. I sold my condo and my car. I gave all my furniture and paraphernalia to charity. I found a safari-guiding school, Ulovane, outside of Port Elizabeth, South Africa. I filled a backpack with my last remaining personal items and moved to Africa.

I have been living and working in Africa as a guide for five years now. Like Barry predicted, I love every waking moment. I arise every day looking forward to new adventures among Africa's wildest animals, unforgettable landscapes, and captivating people. My days, however, would not be nearly as fulfilling without my clients who come from all over the world seeking adventure in a place that breaks one's heart with its suffering and its beauty—a place impossible to forget.

THIS is Africa is a compilation of stories that represent just a few of the innumerable, unforgettable experiences I've had in Africa. I could spend another five years writing about all the others. Perhaps one day I will. For now, I am content following my heart in a place that is all about the heart.

I hope *THIS is Africa* will inspire those wanting to come to Africa to make the trip of their lifetime.

Mat Dry, 2011

CHAPTER ONE

MORTALITY MOMENTS

NKOSI: MY JEWISH MOTHER'S WORST NIGHTMARE

It has occurred to me several times throughout my guiding career that every safari guide, as an integral part of his or her training, should have to live with a Jewish mother for at least a month. For those not familiar with the ways of a Jewish mother, they are the best worriers and potential problem solvers in the world. They are masters of the if-then hypothetical, understanding with relative intelligence, cause and effect on another plane. For example, "If you don't put on a sweater, because I'm cold, then you will catch a cold." Or, "If you don't put on clean underwear in the morning and you have a fatal accident, then everyone will think you're an unclean person when they strip your corpse." These are analogously indispensable when considering the possibilities of walking people through a dangerous game area. Of course, no Jewish mother would have ever allowed her child to become a walking safari guide in the first place. Maybe a lawyer or doctor for a walking safari guide, but definitely *not* a safari guide...

"Mat, come in for Ben" comes through my handheld radio.

"Mat standing by, Ben," I answer. I have just asked to find out where Norman, our dominant bull elephant, is just for good measure. I had seen him about three and half hours previously a mile and a half away, browsing lazily across the river but not since.

We are walking in the middle of Platt, an open area covered by flowing red grass, Southern Harvester Termite mounds, unseen aardvark holes, and surrounded by thicket. Ahead of us at about two hundred yards is the only tree, a giant pom-pom-looking thing called a Thorny Karee. With the .375 rifle weighing heavily in my left hand, I am leading my fellow Ulovane students—Alex, Sally, Jon, Drew, and my mentor, Colin—all in a straight, compact line. I know where all the dangerous game on the whole reserve are, excluding Norman and white rhino, Nkosi, whose name means "king" in Xhosa.

My call to find out where Nkosi is several minutes earlier also proved to be fruitless. We had seen Nkosi three hours previously at the beginning of our walk. He had been with one of the females and her calf by Ulovane Pan, about seven hundred yards right of our present location, down a steep, thicket-encrusted hill. He had been decidedly unhappy as the female had rejected his amorous advances due to the presence of her most recent offspring.

When we first came onto Platt from two other sightings necessary for my training (the buffalo herd and two other rhinos) at Eland Loop, I could see the female and her calf five hundred yards to our right. They were at the edge of Platt, very near to the hill going down to Ulovane Pan. I made the assumption that because we couldn't see Nkosi, he must be very near them in the thicket. As I mentioned earlier, Nkosi liked to shadow them for the outside chance she might have a change in loins for his advances. With my Jewish-mother senses tingling, I chose to walk in the middle of Platt, on the road there, so we wouldn't be surprised by Nkosi if indeed he was in the thickets to either side of Platt. The wind was also blowing in our favor as it was coming from their position and heading slightly forward and to our left.

"Channel four, Mat," Ben scratches through the handheld again. I look down to turn the knob to channel four, but never get to do it. Alex's voice barks behind me, "Mat!" His tone alone rivets me in my tracks. I look up. A hundred yards in front and to our left, Nkosi strides out from behind the Thorny Karee. Adrenaline rockets into my system, and my hand crushes the rifle in a vise-like grip.

I don't need to tell anyone to stop, but I do. We are all frozen to our spots, roots of terror growing into the ground from our feet. The reality of our situation hits me like...well, a charging rhino. My assumption that Nkosi was with the female and calf was wrong—very wrong. Jewish Mother 101, for once, has failed me. Nkosi snorts and stares toward us; he knows we are here. His radar-like ears try to lock onto what his poor eyes are having a hard time seeing.

"Back up slowly..." I order the group. I flip the rifle to my right shoulder but do not cock it. I watch Nkosi like he is the only thing my eyes will ever see again. Everyone begins backing up from the road, our twelve legs swishing through the red grass. Nkosi's ears shoot forward toward our noise. I glance back behind me to see if there is cover for us. Aside from a miniscule bush that wouldn't shelter a sparrow, there is nothing but the vast sea of grass around us, a vast sea harboring aardvark holes big enough to fit *both* legs in.

The closest thicket is two hundred yards to what was our right. I start to employ The Schwartz in my head: *Nkosi, just stay there as we swish away. Just look at us and let us go. No harm, no foul.* The Schwartz doesn't work. In fact, Nkosi does the unthinkable. He breaks into a trot, beelining for us.

Something bursts in my head: *Holy sh-t, holy sh-t, holy sh-t! This is happening! Rhino, rhino, rhino! Charges sixty feet per second, sixty feet per second! What have I learned? Yell "Stand still! Don't run! Stay behind me!" Then, yell and scream. If the rhino charges to ten yards, shoot it.*

5

I turn my head to yell my instructions and see our necessary single-file line has fallen into utter chaos. Behind me, there are bodies scattered, moving all over the place. Even more interesting, Colin, who has been in this situation a number of times, has turned around toward the thicket. Watching Nkosi over his shoulder, he has begun a trot of his own. A very quick trot.

As everyone knows, you are never supposed to run, but I trust Colin. After all, he has a SKS (Special Knowledge and Skills) Qualification in Viewing Potentially Dangerous Animals (in doing exactly what we have been doing for the past three hours). Meanwhile, Nkosi is closing the distance. He is a tank, six and a half feet high at the shoulder and three tons, and he is determined to find his target: us. He is fifty yards away. *If my Jewish mother could only see me now.* Sudden Cardiac Death for her, no question about it.

The strongest impulse I have ever had in my thirty-six years courses through me. I want to turn around and run for my f–king life. Somehow, I don't. I want to cock the rifle, but also do not. I can't run with a chambered weapon. And, although Nkosi is coming after us, he isn't charging. At least, not yet. I turn back to yell "Follow Colin!", but see everyone has already made that command decision. They're moving at the closest thing to a "not-run" one can get. I lift the rifle to aim position. I point it back behind me and begin a "not-run" of my own.

"Not-running" through a sea of red grass, dodging aardvark holes, and looking back over one's shoulder down the length of a high-powered rifle at a rapidly approaching rhino is not as easy as it sounds. When one doesn't have a choice, however, it happens automatically, in fast-forward. At about fifty yards from the thicket, Colin fades left at an angle to the thicket. This will keep us within the grass for an extra fifty yards, like Moses leading the Jews alongside the Promised Land. It is a move whose wisdom I don't recognize, but I am in no position to argue. I am now backup, covering us should Nkosi pick up his already considerable pace. In our hasty retreat, Colin has cleverly surmised that if we can keep the distance between us *and* get out of the wind blowing our scent to Nkosi, he will stop following.

I stare at the rapidly approaching line of trees that marks our safety like a drowning man stares at the shore. That stare, however, is a luxury as I have to flick my eyes back at Nkosi inexorably closing in on us. I can hear the crunch of his feet on the ground, and my hand itches on the bolt to cock the rifle. *Almost there, almost there, almost there.* Nkosi rumbles once, and all heads turn back to see how close he is. "Still coming! Keep going!" escapes my lips. He's as close to us as we could ever hope a rhino *not* to be.

Colin hits the tree line followed quickly by the rest of us. We clamber behind the sparse group of trees and shrubs and hold ourselves perfectly still. We look back, ready to duck deeper into the bush if necessary. Nkosi, thankfully, stops. At forty yards (three seconds at full speed) from us, our being stationary behind the trees and the wind no longer blowing our scent to him, he can no longer see, hear, or smell us. Just in case we didn't get the memo on how impressive he is, Nkosi snorts and turns sideways, giving us a lateral display. We don't need any reminding. He has empirically proven he is the most impressive thing we have all seen in our entire lives. For me, it is the greatest impression made on me since my circumcision.

We follow the tree line and stop again at about two hundred yards from Nkosi. He still looks massive, a snapshot straight out of pre-history. We all look at one another, the color coming back into our faces. Nervous laughter erupts. Some of us check our undies for involuntary mishaps. I relax my hand on the rifle. My forearm has cramped from my adrenaline-filled grip. Spreading my fingers and rubbing my forearm feels like Heaven.

Everyone starts chattering at once, but I am quiet. I am flooded with the Jewish-mother what-ifs. What if he had been charging?

What if someone had fallen down? What if I had fallen down? What if I had to choose between Nkosi's life and ours?

Like all Jewish mother what-ifs, there is usually little comfort in the "thens." If I, as a guide, am to walk in the wilds of Africa and a rifle is necessary for protection, then I must be willing to kill an animal whose only crime would be meeting me and my clients in the proverbial "wrong place at the wrong time." That would be heartbreaking.

As we trek back to Ulovane, I come to the rather unsettling conclusion: *if* I am going to be a walking-safari guide, *then* the only real solution for me is to do walking safaris in places where a rifle isn't required or allowed. *Right*. Try selling that one to my Jewish mother.

SCRABBLE THIS

Dr. Samia Jamal is a lovely anesthesiologist, just about to turn thirty, from Winchester, England. This trip to Africa is her first in many ways: it is the first time on a camping trip; it is the first time traveling on an overland truck; and it is the first time she is traveling with her four, twenty-something, English friends—Kay, Liz, Sunny, and Carla. Of the five of them, only two have ever put up a tent. It is certainly her first adventure into the Okavango Delta or any wilds of any place where there is a host of animals and situations that would most assuredly kill her if given the right circumstance— circumstance, for example, like playing Scrabble in the shade of a rain tree during our rest time between hikes…

We all sit hunched over the Scrabble board on our one-foot-tall stools. Samia lazes on her sleeping mat on the ground between Steve, a twenty-six-year-old American to my right, and Kay, who sits directly across from me intensely involved in our ruthless game. Sunny, to my left, is in cahoots with Kay as Kay is in cahoots with both Samia and Steve. Their mission is to defeat me as humiliatingly as possible as I have been somewhat shamelessly winning our games every day on the truck during the long hours between destinations.

As I look down at the letters in my hand, I come to the rather unsavory realization that I am pretty much screwed. I am not going to come out on top in this game. Sunny, a teacher from Birmingham and also one of the funniest people I have ever met (known to break out into sudden song from *The Lion King,* fully backed by a lion dance) puts down her letters and says emphatically, "Thirty-two points! What do you think of *that one*, Dry-man ?"

I look at the word and grin. "Won't do you any good; I've got a seven-letter word (an extra fifty points guaranteeing me the win) sitting here ready for a home right next to yours."

She, Kay, Samia, and Steve exchange frowns. Sunny says it for them: "You suck." I snicker back at her. I can let them sweat it out for two more turns. We settle in for Kay's turn, which usually lasts a glacial period of time. We are deep in concentration when the uninvited guest appears.

I see it first. All it requires for me is a shift of my eyes from the letters in my hand to the ground. It's sleek, gray head stops a foot beneath my hands, right between my feet. Its black, forked tongue flicks in and out of its mouth twice before I can identify the species. *Mfezi.* My blood turns to ice. Samia, with her snake-eye view, is not five feet from the snake, a Mozambique Spitting Cobra.

She sucks in her breath. The others look at her and her face frozen with terror. I watch their eyes move from her face to the cobra beneath me. I know what's coming even before they do it. "Don't move," I hiss through clenched teeth, as loud as I can without moving any part of my body. They freeze instantly.

The cobra shoots its three-inch head up to the height of my knee and spreads its hood. I know this reptile is capable of sending a spray of venom through the holes in the front of its fangs a distance of up to nine feet and over three feet wide. That would encompass everyone present, with Samia getting the bulk of it. Within seconds, the venom can cause impaired vision with mind-numbing pain. Ultimately, blindness ensues if not flushed from the eyes.

The snake sways steadily there as I consider grabbing it by the back of the head. *Really* bad idea. If I don't grab it perfectly, I will be bitten. Mfezi have both cytotoxic and neurotoxic venom and, if the neurotoxic venom doesn't shut down the nervous system, the cytotoxic venom will cause massive necrosis of the flesh that can lead to deadly secondary infection. Being bitten this far from civilization (and antivenom) is pretty much certain death. If I do grab it perfectly, it still may be able to cover the onlookers with venom. Eyes open with terror are perfect receptacles for sprayed cobra venom.

One one-thousand, two one-thousand, three one-thousand...

Again, the cobra tests the air with its forked tongue, dragging our molecules into his Organ of Jacobson housed in the roof of its mouth. It is an organ of taste and smell combined, allowing it to determine if he has inadvertently entered into a hostile environment and should start spraying. I'm praying its organ is malfunctioning today. We stare at the cobra as if it is Medusa turning us to stone. It is the longest three seconds of our lives.

Perhaps sensing the rather unwelcome energy above and around it, but no threat of movement, it collapses its hood. It slowly sinks to the ground. It deftly flicks its head around my Achilles tendon. With far too little urgency, its five-foot length goes across my heel, around a tree to our left, and disappears into the thicket.

I look at the others wide-eyed with wonder and a huge grin stretches across my face. "That was AWESOME!" I yell. No one is breathing. I hold my hand up. "High five, everyone." They stare at me as if I have grown a couple more heads. With a symphonic gush of air, they expel their breath. Samia immediately turns her head to hide the tears that the adrenaline has most assuredly brought to her eyes.

Sunny raises an eyebrow at me in her characteristic, scolding way. "Please tell me that wasn't what I think it was."

"Depends on what you think it was. Did you think it was a Mozambique Spitting Cobra?" I ask. She and the others can see my barely controlled enthusiasm at the whole experience.

"I hate you, Dry-man," she says, deadpan.

I turn my attention to Samia. "You alright, Doctor?" She nods. *Her first brush with mortality.*

Kay looks at me seriously. "Is it too late to go back to civilization?" Everyone laughs.

"Don't worry. The lesson to learn here is that it was more scared of us. It could have sprayed you all with its venom, but what did it choose to do? It chose to go on its merry way, hurting no one." Again, they stare at me as if I've lost my marbles.

"You're a little too safari-guidish for me," says Steve. "I gotta go change my shorts…"

EXECUTION VALLEY

I am two weeks into my new job as a guide at Leeuwenbosch Lodge, Amakhala, in South Africa. I have passed my First Level and need ninety days of guiding to help complete my FGASA's Second Level. This translates, in practical terms, to another five and a half months at Leeuwenbosch.

Looking out over the area known as Impala Flats, I'm seeing a guide's greatest wish fulfillment on a game drive that has lacked the biggest of the famous Big Five— elephant, lion, buffalo, black rhino (although some will settle for white), and leopard. Even though this family of four with me (father, Jim, a self-confessed adventurer who once ran with the bulls in Pamplona; mother, Carie; daughter, Laura, fourteen; and son, Merrick, ten) has been on many safaris in Southern Africa, they still want to see some of the Big Five today. It is their last day of safari on Amakhala.

To our left, 150 yards away, three bull elephants are having a playful tussle in a copse of trees. Across the valley, the family herd of eleven and a quarter (a several-week-old infant) elephants heads toward the area known as the Kloofs (deep valleys in the north-east of Amakhala) for their winter evening's retirement. Just to our right, a mother white rhino and her calf are mixing it up with the family herd of fourteen buffalo out on the plain. I smile in the front seat. We can have it *all*. The only issue at hand is how to make the most of our present position in our given amount of time. I've been scolded every day for being tardy. My over-curricular exploration of the reserve with our guests is not as rewarding for my bosses as it is for me and my guests. I am supposed to bring the guests back by seven o' clock so they can get ready for drinks in the bar at eight o' clock, and then dinner is served at 8:45 p.m. The earliest I've returned in the past two weeks is 7:25 p.m. "I can't help it. I love it out there," I tell my new bosses.

"Help it," they tell me.

It is half past six, and I am already late. It will take at least a half hour to get back to the lodge from here, and that's without visiting the possible sightings before us. I know the bulls shouldn't be approached too closely as they are deep into the fourth or fifth round of wrestling one another. I decide instead to explain from our present location the cultural meme of bull elephants instructing younger bulls in the ways of growing up.

"One of the great and possibly most hazardous ignorances people may have when starting a reserve is their lack of knowledge about elephant culture. If you bring a young teenage bull to a reserve who has not spent a lot of time with older bulls, he may become very aggressive toward anything and everything. Young bulls need to take out their teenage energies, like any unruly teenager. It is up to the larger bulls to keep them disciplined. This disciplining will also teach the young bulls skills they will need in the future when the time comes for them to do battle for mating rights. If a mature bull (in his twenties on up) is not present, the young bull may decide that a rhino, buffalo, or even a Land Rover with passengers will be a good thing to wrestle with.

"Anyway, what first?" I ask enthusiastically. Judging by their expressions, I can see we are as close to the bulls as they want to get. Not visiting them at all will save us a little time, of course. The buffalo and rhino as a single unit, however, seem to be heading into the thickets by the river. I make the command decision aloud to let the elephants head into the Kloofs and see the buffalo and rhino first. They concur unanimously.

The only thing keeping us from racing over to where we can intercept the grazing herd is my ex-tentmate at Ulovane, Drake. He is heading toward them from another vantage point five hundred yards out. Getting there before us, he will have first rights to the sighting and will, thus, be in control of it.

I call Drake on the radio requesting to share the sighting. "Hello, my friend," he says. "Of course you can join us."

We buzz over and, within five minutes, our guests are exchanging pleasantries. The animals are gently grazing at forty yards out and moving south from our location.

"You wanna get a little closer?" I smile to Drake. He knows what an amazing experience it is to have these animals moving, feeding, and breathing around the vehicles. It is something neither of us wants our guests to miss.

"I'll follow you," he says congenially.

I take the road that aims around the herd to a point two hundred yards in front of them. We arrive at our destination fifty yards ahead of their grazing. Drake and I gurgle our vehicles to a stop and switch off our engines. "Just stay very quiet and still if the animals come near the vehicles. If they are closer than fifteen feet, please don't use your cameras," I remind them.

Thirty yards, twenty yards, ten yards... The rhinos and the buffalo approach us as if we are just another part of the environment. The excitement in the trucks is electric. "How cute is that?" Laura whispers and points. From here, we can see perfectly the week-old buffalo calf hassling his mother between her back legs for an udder.

He is a chocolate brown and easily identified against the others' black hides and muscular bulk. Compared to the baby rhino of one year not five yards from him, he is a brown speck. He stops and looks at us as the cameras whir and click. He looks at his mother for instruction about these big green creatures making strange noises. She goes right on grazing. After about ten seconds of quizzical scrutinizing, he bucks and cavorts back to the cover of his mother's back legs.

We sit and listen to the animals tearing at the grass, the rhinos with their square lips, the buffalo with their thick, muscular tongues. We can almost *feel* their deep, rhythmic breathing as they surround us. Against the backdrop of the fiery reds, oranges, and yellows of the setting sun, it is a perfect example of why we go on safaris. Although we are safely ensconced in the safety of a mechanized vehicle, we are nonetheless a part of the herd, another player in the theater of this environment.

Daggaboy (meaning Mudboy, as bull buffalo are called due to their wont to roll themselves in mud to rid themselves of parasites and cool off), our largest and dominant bull on Amakhala, brings up the rear. Usually solitary, Daggaboy joins the herd occasionally when passion inspires him to do so. He eyes us and trudges his one-ton weight forward.

He is no more than three feet from the left-front of the vehicle when he stops to look at us. I can feel the adrenaline begin its surge through my veins. I know behind me they are feeling the same thing as Laura sucks in her breath. I again hold my hand to my lips. Although very accustomed to vehicles, Daggaboy, like most buffalo, is unpredictable. He could easily jump up on the Landie and gore someone near the edge if he were so inclined.

He snorts once as he passes by, his massive, horned head swinging side to side. He clomps back to Drake directly behind me. The whole group breathes a sigh of relief and awe. I nod to Jim to continue his photo spree. I pull out my camera and snap a few photos of the animals. It is the best buffalo sighting I have ever had, and my first of the calf.

"Are you guys happy?" I ask, glowing. They nod and grin like a family of Cheshire cats. "To the elephants?" I ask. More smiles. I give them the thumbs up. We wave to Drake and his guests as I pull away.

For a moment I am envious of Drake. He's already seen everything we want to see. His lodge, Woodbury, however, is visible on a beautiful cliff overlooking our present position, not fifteen minutes away. No scolding for him tonight. I, on the other hand, am heading for Scold City as we still have the elephant herd to see.

I head up over a hill to the road that leads to Terry's Crossing. Terry's Crossing is a man-made dam built to cross this stretch of the thirteen miles of Bushman's River, which winds its serpentine length through the reserve. From there, Langkloof Road runs into the Kloofs, and the area known as Execution Valley. It is so named to remind those who go in there and find themselves between the cliffs and among the elephants or rhino that they should kiss their butts good-bye.

Usually, at sunset in the winter, many of the guides will take their passengers to the hill just south and above Terry's Crossing. There we have the perfect position to do Sundowners (drinks and snacks). Not forty yards below us, the elephants enter the valleys using a donga (erosion ditch) that runs parallel to Langkloof Road.

Langkloof Road runs five hundred yards along the donga before the donga shallows itself to the road. A hundred yards in front of that, the road splits three-way, left into Execution Valley, straight to the highlands of Vredeland above the valleys, or right, which is the continuation of Langkloof (and the shortest way home). If we can see the elephants and get down Langkloof, we will have our cake and gobble it, too. We may even get back to the lodge by 7:25 p.m. I can at least say I'm trying.

I won't take Execution Valley or the highland road as that will get me back to the lodge sometime next week. I know that I can't take Langkloof if the elephants have gone that way. Langkloof Road passes between two sheer cliffs with a fifteen-yard-wide, five-yard-deep, thicket-encrusted donga on its north side. Getting stuck in there with them is assured death.

The only other option is to skip the elephants, hang a right, and take another route. That will get us back to the lodge a little later than Langkloof, but without the elephants. I know the family will be as disappointed as I will be.

We cross Terry's Crossing, and I turn off the vehicle. "We'll just sit here for a couple minutes and listen to what they're doing, guys," I say.

"Great!" is Jim's response. I can tell they are excited. So am I. We sit and listen. Not a minute into our listening, we are rewarded. A powerful trumpeting reaches us from the depths of the Kloofs.

I look back at the family, and they are frozen with eyes wide open. I raise my eyebrows. "Impressive, no?" The kids nod their heads, acquiescing one hundred percent. Several trumpets echo down to us over the next ten seconds. "Something's spooking the family herd," I state excitedly.

I am more than a little curious to find out what is making them make such a racket. I consider the wisdom of going in there. I decide that we can get in there safely and, if we have to reverse, I just need to reverse straight to be safe. I tell them the strategy. "If it even seems like the elephants are close to the road, we will have to reverse back here. There is only one way in and out of Langkloof. Everyone alright and understand?" I ask.

"Absolutely," Jim says unperturbed. He digs himself into the seat for the adventure ahead. Carie looks skeptically at him. I can tell she is thinking, *You didn't have kids when you went running with the bulls in Pamplona.*

I smile at them. "Here we go."

We inch our way down Langkloof Road, listening intently. The smell of elephant is strong in our nostrils. I stop the vehicle every twenty-five yards to glance down to our left into the donga. The last thing we need is to run into the elephants where the donga meets Langkloof. We hear nothing but the wind. Bit by bit, and stop after stop, we work our way down Langkloof.

We can still hear an occasional trumpet or two, but it sounds far in front and up the hill on our right. No danger there. As we reach the tri-fork in the road, a deep stomach rumble reaches us, and I frown. It sounds like it is coming from Langkloof.

"Sh-t," I mutter under my breath. It looks like we're taking the middle road up to Vredeland to make a U-turn and go back toward Terry's Crossing.

"Sorry guys," I say. "We can't take the shortcut home as it seems like the elephants are down there. Too risky." The kids breathe a sigh of relief. As I turn the vehicle, a roaring trumpet echoes in the valley from far up on the hill. I stop the vehicle and pull out my binoculars. I spy the herd at least eight hundred yards up on the hill in thick vegetation. Cupha, the herd matriarch, stands on a small outcrop, her ears wide open. She releases another trumpeting roar out over the valleys like an angry queen. Some of the other elephants behind her in the trees join her. With the sunset sky beyond them, it is an unforgettable image.

"What are they doing, Mat?" Carie asks, frightened.

"I don't know," I respond. "The one making most of the noise is Cupha, the herd matriarch. I've never seen her so worked up before. Maybe the new baby is misbehaving and running around in the bush up there. I can tell you the only thing more dangerous than an angry bull elephant is a mother elephant protecting its baby."

"Wow!" is their awed response. "She *really* seems upset."

"She sure does," I agree.

I count the elephants through the binoculars: one, two, three… seven, eight. I know there should be eleven plus the baby, but the vegetation is thick. If Cupha and the herd are all the way up there, the other three couldn't possibly be down here in the valleys. Elephants will not split up the herd for safety reasons. The herd takes care of its own. *Always*. I hand the kids my binoculars. "Good news, guys," I smile. "We can take Langkloof Road and be back almost on time."

They aren't listening to me. Their eyes are stuck on the herd far above us. Jim snaps photo after photo of Cupha and the herd against the crepuscular sky. I'm feeling good about this. They have been able to see the herd in an amazing way. I can also see they wouldn't want to get any closer to them. It is a win-win situation. *With my expert decision making and only two weeks on the job, I am a guiding hero. We got to do it all,* I think to myself.

"Are we ready, guys?" I ask them, glowing with triumph. They shake their heads absently as they stare up at Cupha still trumpeting above us. In my mind, they are trumpets of triumph echoing across Amakhala, heralding our return home after a brilliant campaign. I am a *moron*.

I roll down the hill and take the left onto the road going into Langkloof Valley, where it is significantly darker. As we roll into the chilling shadows between the valley walls, the smell of elephant is still very strong. It is almost palpable. I shiver and pull my coat tighter around my neck. *Just enjoy the ride home,* I think to myself.

I am lost in a reverie, thinking how I look forward to being late tonight. This was a great day and the perfect end to this lovely family's four days at Leeuwenbosch. I know the family will give a glittering report about the day, and all will be forgiven. I am a hero to my guests and, thus, a hero for the lodge. Two minutes into my reverie, I am rudely interrupted by the terrible reality of my stupidity.

We roll past a bush just at the lip of the donga. My peripheral vision catches movement to the right. I turn my head and look directly into the eyes and open ears of the five-month-old baby elephant. He shakes his little elephant head and lets out what would be an adorable little trumpet, if it didn't cause a revelatory explosion in my brain. Embarrassingly, "Oops" is what escapes my lips.

It is the ear-deafening roar from the much bigger bush thirty feet down from the baby that confirms, with no uncertain clarity, what has occurred. Cupha and the herd are up on the hill freaking out because she is missing at least two of the three elephants down here in the valley with us . The family behind me screams almost as loud as I do. With adrenalized ferocity, I drop into second gear and jam on the accelerator. I'm pretty sure the only thing that keeps the family from being launched up and out of the Land Rover is that they all have already grasped the railings in front of them with their own adrenalized ferocity.

As we fishtail past the bush housing Mama pachyderm, she twists her furious, shaking head through the bush and lets loose another earth-quaking roar. I'm pretty sure the tip of her trunk is touching my eardrum. *Six can play that game.* We respond with more terrified shrieking of our own.

We don't make it very far. Not thirty yards past Mama and baby, I come to a screeching halt. Once again, I'm pretty sure the only thing keeping the family from being launched over my head is their death-grips on the railings. Twenty yards up on our right, another trembling bush gives off another ear-blasting trumpet. *Yup.* Eight elephants up there and three elephants down here make eleven. It occurs to me that the only way I won't be a total failure is if we all don't die.

My adrenaline kicks in double-time as I try not to panic. I am trained for situations like this. I think of the number one rule of guiding: Don't be an idiot and get into compromising situations. *Rule number one: no longer applicable. Rule number two: think, you idiot!*

I switch off the vehicle so as not to offend the elephants anymore. I turn my head slightly and hold my finger to my lips. The family has saucer-eyes all around. I turn back to the steering wheel and weigh my options at light-speed: Do I back up and risk pissing off the already angry mother even more? Do I race forward and try and get past the other unknown elephant, which may very well be the new mother with the ten-day-old infant and probably the most dangerous animal on the planet today? Do I sit there with my terrified guests and wait until the elephants wander off?

I answer my own questions with what I'm sure is greater light-speed. If I back up, not only is the road barely wide enough for the vehicle and unmanageable, but also the already angry mother may see that as an attack and kill us. If I sit there with terrified, screaming guests and the elephants come into the road with us between them, then they may feel threatened as a team and kill us. The only option, I reason, is to risk the elephant in front of us *not* being the mother of the infant. Just step on the accelerator and jet on by.

All is too silent in the valley. I know the elephants are waiting to see what we do. As I turn back to the family, I need to look like I deal with this all the time. From the waist up (which is all the family can see) I am as cool as a penguin in an Antarctic winter. Below, my foot is shaking on the clutch like it's having its own epileptic fit.

"Listen guys," I whisper with perfect false confidence, "I am going to go pretty fast past this elephant ahead. Please be as quiet as possible, stay close to the center of the vehicle, and hold on, okay?" I've never seen such an ambivalent group of people. I'm certain the only thing keeping them from killing me themselves is the fact they think they need me to keep the elephants from killing *them*.

"She is going to trumpet at us and may even burst her head through the bushes there, but we'll go right on by. She doesn't want a physical confrontation any more than we do. We'll be fine. Okay?" I can almost hear their necks creaking as they nod in the affirmative.

I look at the road ahead. The walls of the valley seem to be closing in. The road appears just wider than a tightrope. To make this even more difficult, thirty yards past the elephant, the road curves precariously to the right. *A learning curve.* To my panicky eyes, it looks like a ninety-degree angle. *Maybe the universe should put a couple speed bumps in the road just for good measure,* I can't help but think. I almost break the key in the ignition as I start the Landie. "Hold on!" I jam it into gear, and I gun it like I'm flying an F-16 off a carrier.

We shoot forward toward the bush. Fifteen feet from it, the bush shakes like it is ready to blast off. A roar like a hundred lions bursts from it. If I could actually hear in my right ear after the roar of the previous elephant, it would be the loudest thing I've ever heard. As we rocket by, I refuse to look at what must be an enormous head, huge ears, and death-dealing tusks not a foot from the side of my head. No one is screaming louder than the elephant as far as I can tell. We shoot toward the curve.

They say there are no atheists when escaping an angry elephant at 35 mph around a bend. Never has there been a truer statement. Someone (probably me) is yelling, "Please, God! Please, God!" as the elephant's final trumpet propels us into the turn.

I pump the brakes as we go into it and make the curve on two wheels, possibly one. I'm sure we're pulling four or five G's when we shoot out of the curve and down the road. If the family had been playing the game "corners," there wouldn't have been an uncracked rib among the four of them. A good five hundred yards down the road, and out of the valley, I stop the Landie. We all exhale a cloud of adrenaline and endorphins simultaneously. We sit for a moment, no one moving.

I unhook my fingers from the steering wheel. A huge grin spreads across my face. *That was AWESOME!* I immediately quash the grin and slowly turn around to look at my guests behind me. "Everyone alright?" I ask calmly, concerned.

Three of four have sparkly eyes and huge grins. Carie, the odd one out, looks like I may have to give her CPR in a second or two. Laura laughs. "That was like a Disney ride!"

"Yeah! Yeah!" Merrick cries.

Disney, my ass, I think, *but I'm glad they enjoyed it.* I look at Jim. He looks back at me with a slight grin on his face, nodding. I know he's thinking, *Screw Pamplona.* He puts an arm around Carie; she is okay.

I allow the smile to creep back onto my face. "Anyone want to go back and do it again?" Their "No!" is instantaneous.

"Answer me one more question, guys," I laugh. "Anyone else soil their pants besides me?"

When they are leaving, we hug like family members parting ways. Safari has a way of bringing strangers together. So does shared, near-death experiences on a safari. I can't help but ask them what their favorite thing was after their whopping eight game drives. The answer: "The elephants in the valley."

I smile broadly. "Mine, too."

CHAPTER TWO

TIA

SOMETHING KILLED

When he introduces himself, Greg exclaims with a glint in his eye and a wide grin on his face, "I want to see something killed!" There is a titter of laughter and more nods of agreement than not. It is a very common reply when I ask passengers what they most want to see on their adventure through Africa. It is not hard to understand the desire to witness a kill. It is one of Nature's most dramatic visual spectacles. A frown tugs at the corner of my lips. I know the truth about witnessing a kill. For most, it is a wish they ultimately wish they had not made.

Not wanting to scare my passengers on the first day of their trip, I don't tell them the kill one sees on the National Geographic Channel is usually accompanied by a dramatic soundtrack covering the worst parts of the kill: the screaming of the prey-animal mixed with the savage growling of the predators, the tearing of flesh, and the crunching of bone. Most animals sound like a screaming child as they are being brought down and consumed. There is much that is awesome about a kill, but very little of it can be construed as pleasurable. "Be careful what you wish for here in Africa, Greg," I say as light-heartedly as possible.

It is morning in the Namibian desert. The sun has just risen, bathing the stark vastness of the Namib-Naukluft in a golden–orange brilliance. Staring out the windows at the glow of the morning desert, the passengers are still waking up. Perhaps they are looking more forward to being back in the arms of civilization in the seaside town of Swakopmund after five days than seeing the sunrise glow of the desert. The wilds of Africa have not yet been wild enough for them in savagery's terms, but certainly so in the lack of civilization's amenities.

Nick slows the truck to a standstill, and I leap to my feet. He knows to stop if there is ever an animal by or in the road, especially reptiles. By the cloud of dust in the middle of road in front of us, it is evident there is a much greater drama unfolding than a reptile making the hell-bent dash for survival.

Ahead is a whirlwind of sand created by two battling Oryx. I can see immediately this is not a friendly sparring match between these two beautiful antelope bulls. The speed, dexterity, and force with which they are attempting to stake each other with their spear-like horns portray these two mean business. *Lethal* business.

"This is not something that happens very often, guys, let alone seen," I say to the passengers as they, too, jump from their seats. "Two antelope fighting to the death is much rarer than most believe. Most animals, most of the time, solve their dominance issues with rituals and almost no physical contact." Nick switches off the vehicle so we can sit and watch.

The two animals, magnificent creatures in the prime of their lives, are utterly exhausted. They may have been going at it all night. The muscles beneath the animals' skin writhe like subcutaneous serpents. Their deep, powerful breathing is almost tangible in the truck as they press their bulk, slash their heads sideways and around, and try to impale each other. The harsh clacking of the horns as they deftly parry one another's savage thrusts makes some of the passengers jump. Then, of course, there is the blood.

The horns of an Oryx can be over a meter long. Straight and dagger-sharp at the ends, they could easily skewer a foe or an enemy attempting to do it harm. There is an account of a lion, having attempted to make a meal of an Oryx, finding itself impaled on the horns. Unable to extricate themselves from this impalement, the two creatures died in this most intimate and horrible of entanglements.

During this battle, one of the Oryx has snapped his horn in half, possibly in the inch-thick skin of his foe's neck. It's hard to tell as blood lies like an angry Jackson Pollock painting over the foe's beautiful white, black, and gray coat from a dozen different slashes and stab wounds. This is not quite as stomach-churning as the fact that its horn has, at some point, penetrated the half-unicorned Oryx's lung. With every powerful breath it expels, blood froths from its lips. It is most assuredly going to be the one defeated and killed. It is impossible to look away.

Most sit with their mouths hung open in awe and dismay. It is more than a car wreck. *Much more*. It is the fight for survival that most humans would dread if put in the hooves of such an animal. It makes one wonder what could possibly be worth this battle of blood and certain death. I look at Greg to see if he has received his wish. The look on his face betrays his true feelings, even as he snaps photos of the living carnage. He could begin projectile vomiting at any moment.

I try and soften the horror of the scene. "I know it's tough to see, but this is how Oryx and most animals determine who will pass on his superior genes. If an animal like this cannot defeat a fellow Oryx with strength and prowess, how will he do against a lion or group of hyenas? By fighting like this, they make sure the strongest will survive."

No one is listening.

Sue appears at my shoulder, tears in her eyes. Her hands are pasted to her face, her mouth slightly open in abject revulsion. I know she wants to close her eyes and never see this again. I know she cannot. I know, like everyone riveted to these beautiful animals savaging each other, they will never *not* see this image when they think of their trip through Africa.

Nick, perhaps stirred by an innate want to help a suffering creature, starts the engine and guns it in neutral. The Oryx do nothing to show they have heard it. They actually push and shove each other *closer* to the truck. Desperately, Nick jams on the horn, but to no avail. He finds a gear and jumps the truck toward the antelope gladiators. Some passengers cheer, including Greg.

We are no more than five yards from the dying, desperate animals when Nick stops. They are oblivious to us. They, and their fight for dominance, are each other's entire universe. Sue whimpers next to me, "Please go! Just go…" It is enough. I press the buzzer to let Nick know to get us out of here. He backs the truck from the fixated bulls. He guns the engine, and we tear away.

All bodies and eyes shift to the back of the truck as the Oryx fade in the distance. As the carnage disappears behind us, it is like we have just left a funeral. A few sniffles are heard. Some check their photos as others stare out the window, a deep consternation in their eyes. A few blink their eyes as if incredulous to what they have witnessed.

I look at Greg one last time before sitting down. He fidgets with his camera, his head down. I can't tell if there are tears in his eyes, but I wouldn't be surprised if they are there. I know no photo will ever make him feel better about getting his wish. Yet, these photos and its memories will help him recognize that he was privileged enough to see not only one of the most grim, yet fascinating wonders in Africa's wilds, but in all Nature.

WISA TROUBLE

I have to ask again before I can accept the horrible reality that awaits me. "What?" I ask, looking into Diane's teary-eyed face.

"They say Ah don't have a wisa for Malavi and that Ah need one! Iz dat true? Vat are vee going to do?"

I get that terrible sinking feeling in my stomach when the bad news you just received means worse news. I respond calmly, not unaware of her use of the word "vee." "Let me check my list," I grumble with great trepidation.

I jog back to the truck, remembering my overlanding trainer's story of the time one of his clients, a South Korean who spoke no English, didn't have a "wisa." He and his illustrious client had to go from Chipata's border town three hundred miles back to Lusaka, Zambia, to get it. They then had to retrace the route back to meet the truck where they would stay for three days on Lake Malawi. It took them three and a half days to do it. The rub, of course, is that it is the client's responsibility to get the visa before he, or she, gets to Africa.

"F–k," I say aloud as I check the list. Swiss citizens need a visa. To this point, Diane has been a model passenger and a true pleasure to have on the truck. Likable in many ways, she is a sweet, kind woman who assists disabled and immigrant people to find jobs back in Switzerland. She has been extremely helpful with chores and other passengers' issues. She has already decried her love for Africa, a point for which I naturally give her extra credit.

As I walk back toward her nervously waiting figure in the doorway of the immigration building, her likeability is evaporating by the footstep. This is technically *her* problem, not mine. The idea of going back to Lusaka absolutely horrifies me as I know it will horrify her. Not to mention the truckload of other passengers I have to worry about.

I consider how proficient she is in her English. At thirty-eight, her English isn't bad. It can't be construed as good, either. I remember a statement she made when I first met her five days ago: "Ah take dis trip with ovahlahnding because Ahm afraid to trawel in Ahfricah by mahself. Ah tink dis iz a vanhderful vay of trawel vith ewerybahdy vith ewerybahdy together helping."

I'm on the fence about her when I reach her. "You definitely need a visa," I say seriously. It probably sounds like a death sentence to her. Her shoulders slump. I give her a couple moments to let that sink in before I continue.

"Vaht can Ah do?" she implores with forlorn eyes. *Sh-t.* I'm a sucker for forlorn eyes.

I sigh. "Well, going back to Lusaka will be a nightmare, but that is what people usually have to do. We can ask nicely for them to let you in. If that doesn't work…" The next thought is so abhorrent to me I can barely bring it to my lips. Corruption in Africa is arguably its greatest plague and I certainly don't want to add to it, but going back to Lusaka is unthinkable. "We are going to have to try and bribe the official."

"AH VANT TO KILL DAT FAHKING VOMAN!" she shrieks.

I step back from her, surprised by her vitriol. "What woman?" I ask.

"Dis fahking voman trawel agent who tells me a wisa for Malavi Ah don't need! Ah speak to her fifty times and she tell me Ah don't need a fahking wisa! Ah could kill her!"

It's my turn to be crestfallen. I have to help Diane. She has gone from being perpetrator to victim in one expletive-filled tirade. "It's okay," I say. "We'll figure it out. Come on." I guide her into the immigration office.

I stride up to the immigration window and put on my best I'm-very-confused-can-you-help-me look. "My client says she needs a visa?"

He looks at me, knowing I know she needs a visa. "Yes. You will have to go back to Lusaka and get the visa there," he states, stoically.

I lean closer to the window. "Is there *some* way, maybe, we can pay a fine and get the visa here? It is an unbearably long way back to Lusaka."

He squints, considering me. His face breaks into a mask of pity. "It is a very, very long way to Lusaka. Maybe I can assist you. Please come around to the back."

We go around "the back" and enter the offices. Diane looks daunted, yet hopeful. "You got a fifty?" I ask her before we enter the official's office. She nods and digs into her bag. She pulls out the fifty and hands it to me. I fold it neatly into a little square. I'm just hoping he doesn't decide that we are trying to bribe him and then try and fine us even more for doing so.

He bids us sit. He sits on the edge of the table in front of us. He eyes us seriously. "You know this is very hard, but I can assist you. We don't do this anymore, but I think in your special case we can make an exception. I will give you a two-day pass to go to Lilongwe and obtain your visa."

"Thank you so much. It is very kind of you, sir," I tell him.

I reach out my hand to shake the official's extended hand, and he expertly slides the fifty from my palm. He flips around the desk like a ballet dancer and fills out a form in thirty seconds. *Very hard stuff.* He flourishes the paper in front of us. "Happy New Year!" he beams and hands Diane the paper. She is ecstatic. For her, it is the best New Year's gift she could have hoped for. I feel like *crap* but would be lying if I said I wasn't relieved.

"It's *what?*" I ask "Dallas" three hours later in Lilongwe, Malawi's capital city. The dubiously-named Dallas, who works the streets of Lilongwe as a money-changer, looks a perfect cross between Will Smith and the Reverend Jesse Jackson. He *acts* like a perfect cross between W.C. Fields and heated popcorn. He stares at me through his alcohol-adjusted, blood-shot eyes. "Yes, my brothaahhh, immigration office is closed today. It is a national holiday because it is the first of the New Year. Happy New Year, my brothaahhh!" He holds out his hand for me to give him the traditional African handshake. I resist the urge to punch him in the face. After exchanging money with him seconds before, assault would be my third illegal action of the day.

"So when do think it will open, Dallas? Tomorrow?" I query, scared to know the answer.

"Most definitely, my brothaahhhh. And lucky for you I know the people there. We will go tomorrow and get the visa in the morning. I will take you and your client. We do good business, don't we my brothaahhh?"

"Yes, Dallas, good business, my friend."

The thought of spending another day in Lilongwe, frankly, makes me want to weep openly in front of my drunken "brothahhh." Although an incredibly friendly place, Lilongwe is stacked with people in a claustrophobic area. For a safari guide in love with open places and African animals, it is categorically not the place for me to be for longer than our usual shopping stint. I keep it together.

"I'll see you in the morning at what time?" I ask.

"Immigration opens at eight o' clock. I will be here on the street corner waiting for you at six. Ha! Ha!"

"Why don't we see you at the immigration office at half past seven, my friend, unless I call you?"

"Okay, half past seven. See you, my brothaahhh!" He hops down from the truck and disappears into a crowd of hawkers. I steel myself for telling Diane the great news.

"Ah vant to fahking kill her!" Diane yells. Yeah, I got that memo. I agree with it one hundred percent. "How long vill it take to get the wisa and vat time leaves the bus?" she asks angrily.

I don't have a clue. "Nick says Dallas is good at getting wisas [I'm starting to say it now!], and we can catch an early bus up north to meet the truck."

She lets out a string of German obscenities and smiles sheepishly. "Ahm sorry! Ahm so disappointed!"

"I'm sure I'm saying the same thing on the inside," I offer to assuage her. "Why don't you pick a place to stay in my Lonely Planet guide?" She sits down to take a look in the book. I pack my bag for a night in this mecca of entertainment and good times.

Ten minutes later, Diane and I, strapped with our bags, wave to the departing truck. I feel like we're being left behind enemy lines. Diane looks as if she is losing her only ticket to freedom. She may be right. Who knows what will happen if they decide for sh-ts and giggles to *not* give her a visa? "Shall we have a little stroll to the hostel?" I ask.

"Ah really think Ah shouldn't have come on dis trip," she mumbles dejectedly. "Did Ah tell about my yellow fewer [fever] waccination story?" She was volunteering at an orphanage in Middle-of-nowhere, South Africa. She had to track down the only doctor within two hundred miles to get the shot. It took her five taxis and a day to finally get it, not to mention a couple hundred dollars.

"Don't worry," I say reassuringly. "We're going to be fine. Tomorrow you'll be on the beach at Lake Malawi soaking up Malawian sunshine!" That seems to brighten her spirits. We set off in the direction we think we should be going.

We come upon a group of policemen and ask them for directions to our hostel, Kiboko Camp. The captain of the group smiles a toothless grin and gestures for us to follow him. Four streets up, we come upon the Kiboko Lodge, a hotel. It is not the place we're looking for. We try to explain to him the confusion but get nowhere. Suddenly, as if materializing from thin air, a pretty Dutch girl appears. "I know where you want to go. I'm staying there, except it's called Mabuya now, not Kiboko."

"Great!" we exclaim and follow her away from the toothless policeman.

We follow her up the street to a T-section. Both Diane and I begin to head left to where the Lonely Planet map seemed to suggest we should go. The chatty Dutch girl, who strangely goes by the Asian name "Ming," points to the right. "I'm sure it's this way," she says emphatically. "I just got dropped off by the hostel, and I'm sure we came from this way." I look at Diane and she shrugs. We follow Ming as she regales us with stories of her couple months of travel around southern Africa.

An hour later, on her sixtieth story, we are asking people on the side of a highway, several miles from the city's center, where the hostel is. Oddly enough, people on both sides of the highway don't know Mabuya or Kiboko Camp. I want to put a FOR SALE sign on Ming to get taxi fare back to where we were supposed to go. I might just be saving Ming's life by selling her, judging by the way Diane is looking at her. I realize, however, I'm the only one to blame. I knew we were going the wrong way. "Dee other vay, vee should have gone," she whispers to me. I gesture for Ming to come back over to us from her fourth inquiry on the other side of the highway.

Ming dances back over to us. "The lady swears that it is just back through this field, across the golf course, and then a couple streets over," she insists merrily.

"No, Ming," I say pointedly. "Any time you ask someone who lives in the area for directions and it takes five minutes for them to tell you, I can assure you they don't know either."

Ming, undaunted by my pessimism, cheers, "It's right over there! I know it!" I turn from her and roll my eyes to Diane who is busy rolling her eyes to me. We agree to follow our Asian-named Dutch friend only because it is, at least, back in the direction I know we need to go.

Several streets over, the only other foreigner we've seen in an hour and a half pulls his car over to us. "Where y'all goin'?" he drawls in what turns out to be an Arkansas accent. I suddenly feel like I'm trapped in a "Twilight Zone" episode. We tell him. "Beck" as he comes to be named, wrinkles his brow. "I may be wrong as I've only been here fahve months, but y'all are in the complete opposite direction than y'all supposed to be. Hop in!"

With a sigh of relief, we clamber inside the vehicle. Twenty minutes later, we arrive at the same spot where we met Ming. I start laughing. Diane, much to her credit, joins me. "This ain't it?" asks Beck.

"I know where we need to go if you're willing to take us," I say, looking at the map in the Lonely Planet guide. "It's a couple streets over."

Ming chimes in, "I think we need to go—"

"Ming," I interrupt her. "You have been very sweet in helping us, but you are officially fired from navigating. No offense."

She's unflappable. "That's okay, I was never hired. Hee! Hee!"

Three minutes later and two streets over, we find Mabuya. We thank Beck for saving us six hours of more hiking around Lilongwe and, undoubtedly, Ming's life. Needless to say, we avoid Ming at the hostel the rest of the night.

Over a decent dinner in the hostel and a nearly incomprehensible phone call with Dallas, Diane and I discuss the next day's events. We are to be up at 6:15 a.m. After breakfast, we will call Dallas at seven o' clock. He will meet us at the immigration office at 7:15 a.m. to be safe. Fortunately, Dallas has informed us, the bus station we need is adjacent to the immigration office.

I'd get the bus tickets at half past seven as Diane and Dallas procured the visa. Then, by eight o' clock we should be on our way to Kande Beach on the *only* Kande Beach-bound bus that leaves Lilongwe each day. It should get us there by noon. If we miss that one, we'll have to wait for a bus to Mzuzu at 12:30 p.m. at a different bus station on the other side of town. That could take up to seven hours and put us at our final destination, after yet another bus, around nine o' clock at night. In other words, if we miss the eight o' clock bus, we'll want to kill ourselves.

"Oh, Ah pray, pray, pray the eight o' clock bus vee make!" Diane says a number of times. I can't get myself to tell her that getting anything through African bureaucracy on your schedule is like asking for Heaven in Hell. I offer an unenthusiastic, "Me, too."

At breakfast, Diane doesn't want to eat anything. Her pasty, white face betrays the fact that she does not feel well. I ask her as much. She drops her eyes to her stomach and waves down with the back of her hands, "Fffffft..."

Perfect. Switzerland's got the runs.

We call Dallas at seven o' clock. He doesn't answer. I swear a lot. We request a taxi to take us the ten minutes to the immigration office. I call Dallas again. *Big surprise,* no answer. I motion for Diane to come with me to the bus station. Diane holds up a finger and plunges into her bag. She pulls her sought-after treasure from its depths. She brandishes a roll of toilet paper in front of me. This may very well be longest day of her life. I have *no* idea.

We enter the office at the bus station. It has all the personality of a bunker in Chernobyl. I ask a stone-faced lady reading a newspaper behind a desk what time the bus leaves, just for good measure. She doesn't look up from her paper. "Eight," she replies with the fervor of a corpse.

"Great. Can I get two tickets, please?" I ask.

"Umhmm." She reaches for her pile of tickets.

"Do you have a toilet, ma'am?" I ask. The woman almost imperceptibly nods at the door. We think it means outside the entrance. Diane races off, toilet paper in hand. I turn to purchase the tickets.

"Eight o' clock doesn't leave from this station," she says with a smirk. She is Medusa. I am stone. *Breathe, Mat. Breathe.*

"Where *does* it leave from, ma'am?" I query, trying not to burst a blood vessel.

She looks down at her paper. "Cross-the-bridge bus station. Look for the AXA bus company sign."

Through gritted teeth, I thank her. That gives us about one minute leeway to catch the bus after getting the visa. Telling Diane will be like rubbing salt in a canker sore. I get an idea.

An agnostic, I am nonetheless praying for Dallas to answer the phone. It is 7:25 a.m. "Please, please, please!" I hear the phone pick up. "*Yes!* Thank you, God," I say.

"Hello?" Dallas slurs into the phone.

"Dallas!" I yell. "It's Mat!" I hear voices in the background. Music one would expect to hear in a strip club floats through the phone.

"*Who?*"

"It's Mat. The tour leader!" *Who? The guy you're supposed to be seeing ten minutes ago with his client.*

"My brothaaahhh! Yes! Yes! How are you, my brothaaahhh?"

Homicidal is how I am. "Where are you, Dallas? We're at the immigration office, which is supposed to open any minute."

"Hakuna matata, my brothaaaahhh. I be there in two minutes! I am very near," he says guiltlessly.

I take a deep breath as I'm about to choke my phone. "Listen, can you be here at half past seven *with* a taxi?" I ask calmly.

"You want me to come there in a taxi?" he yells into my ear.

"Yes, but I want you to tell the taxi driver to stay here while we do the visa. We need to take the taxi to the bus station across the bridge as soon as the visa is done. We have an eight o' clock bus!"

"You want me to come in a taxi at eight o' clock?" he asks, confused.

I am definitely going to kill him after he procures us the visa. "Dallas... *Can...you...be...here...at...7:30...with...a...taxi?*" I ask painfully slowly.

"Yes, my brothaahhh! I see you there at 7:30. No problem."

I flip the phone closed and hang my head. It is the first time I employ the all-encompassing phrase ubiquitously utilized across Africa to explain all things vexing : "TIA." *This is Africa.* I say it aloud, but it doesn't make me feel any better.

"Ah know dat. TIA. Dis iz Ahfrica," Diane offers proudly as she walks up behind me, toilet paper in hand. "Dat iz dee most disgusting toilet in my whole life Ah have seen! She groans like she is still holding her breath.

"Iz Dallas coming?" she asks hopefully. When I inform her of the change of plan, she says, "Ah hope the wisa people come in time."

It is 7:51 a.m. when the first visa official arrives, all smiles and handshakes. Dallas is nowhere to be seen. It doesn't matter. We know we're screwed. There is one hope and that is that the buses also run on Africa time. "Sir, we need to catch an eight o' clock bus. Is there any way for us to do this quickly?"

He doesn't bat an eyelash. "No," he grunts. We wait for an explanation, but he doesn't offer one. With a huge smile, he waves us into the visa offices.

He has Diane fill out several forms. She does it with the alacrity of a woman writing her last will and testament on a plummeting airplane.

"Now, you must go to the office next door and pay for the visa. Seventy dollars American," he states. I nod at her like we are partners on the TV show "The Great Race." We have five minutes to make it happen.

Diane comes back a half hour later, receipt in hand.

Our bus ain't gonna be a half hour late. "Let me guess," I say. "No one in the other office?"

"Yes. He arrives five minutes ago," she replies unemotionally, learning to embrace the horror.

"Half past twelve," I say, which really says it all. She nods, defeated. At least she has her *wisa.*

"You hungry?" I ask.

She wrinkles her face into a mask of disgust. "Ah drink Coke for breakfast iz all. Ah can't eat. It vas dat dinner. Usually my stomach iz wery strong. Wery strange," she adds.

Wery, I think. "Come on," I gesture. "I know a place where you can rest and I can get brunch. We've got four hours to kill."

Fifteen minutes later, we walk into the courtyard of the Lilongwe Hotel. Upon entering the lobby, I get the feeling we have time-warped back to the '70s. I half expect everyone to be wearing bell-bottoms with their collars up around their ears. It is, however, cool and very relaxed in the huge lobby area. I lead Diane to a plush couch against a wall.

She is not looking better after our morning adventure. She lies down on the couch and curls into a fetal position. There's not an injured antelope's chance among a pride of hungry lions we are traveling today. "You want me to get you some toast and tea, Diane?" I ask as compassionately as possible, hiding the huge disappointment I'm feeling.

"No, no, Mat. Dat iz okay. Here Ah vill be fine."

I brunch and sip coffee in the restaurant for two hours, contemplating our options. At 11:20 a.m., I wake Diane from her much-needed nap. It is time to get a taxi across the bridge to the bus station. She looks just this side of death. "You sure you want to travel, Diane? We can stay another night if you want? It's not a problem," I say seriously.

She looks at me with a ferocious intensity. "Not in a million, trillion fahking years" is her answer. Good enough for me.

We head through the lobby with our stuff and out the doors. We pass a tiny, dilapidated fountain. I think maybe a joke will brighten her up. "What do you think of the pool?" I quip. She doesn't even crack a smile. She holds up her hand toward me. *Jeez*, I think, *it's not that bad a joke.* Diane then bolts from me, her other hand covering her mouth. She heads for the nearest bushes. A projectile stream of Coke flies from her mouth. And I thought it couldn't get worse.

I unravel about twenty feet of toilet paper and hand it to her. She wipes her face. "Dis sucks," she says through gritted teeth. *Understatement of the year.*

"Diane, seriously, we don't have to travel today. There's no way you can sit on a bus for eight hours like this. Let's just go tomorrow."

She stands up still wiping her mouth. "Actually, Ah really feel guut!" I look at her like she just threw up her brain. "No, really, Mat. Ah feel soooo much better! Ah should have before done dis!"

I'm pleased that she's pleased. Somehow I'm not convinced it's the end of it. "You're the boss," I say and flag down a cab.

Two minutes from the bus station, now 11:50 a.m., the phone rings. It's Dallas. "Hello, my brothaaahhh! You need a taxi?" he asks. I can still hear the voices and strip-club music in the background. I have no idea what to say to him. I know, like in all Africa, expressing my anger at his no-show would be pointless. "Um, no, Dallas. We're good. We got our visa and are on our way out of town. Thanks for the money exchange. I'll see you next time, my friend."

"You don't want me to get you a taxi?" he asks dejectedly.

"Good-bye, Dallas." I flip the phone closed. I check on Diane in the back of the cab. She clutches a plastic bag to her chest looking wan. "Helpful guy," she says with uncharacteristic sarcasm. I can't help but laugh at that.

We arrive at the bus depot if that is what it can be called. *Malawi has twelve million people crammed into a space the size of Hawaii. Half of them are at this depot.* It is pandemonium incarnate. People, animals, bundles of every size and shape, cars, wheelbarrows, donkey carts—oh yeah, *and buses,* crowd an area half the size of a football field. A Tetris master couldn't rearrange the chaos of this "bus station" in a million years.

Our taxi driver stops the cab just before killing a Lilongwean standing innocently curbside. "That is your bus over there," he points out.

"Thank you, sir," I say, thinking if he hadn't pointed it out, we would never have left this vortex. I hand him two dollars' worth of Malawian kwacha. I help Diane and her plastic bag out of the cab.

Five minutes later I'm standing in front of the bus conductor (the Big Cheese who handles the tickets and crowd control on the bus) with my mouth open. "There is no room," he says again, in case this open-mouthed, silent moron in front of him doesn't speak English. I certainly don't want to believe him. I walk away before I start crying. Public displays of sadness are just as anomalous as anger.

I walk around the bus to where Diane slouches over her bags. The smell of sweating bodies, animal feces, and trash at the bus depot is enough to make one toss brunch. I'm impressed she hasn't started spraying Coke again.

"Um, don't know how to tell you this…" I begin. The tears welling in her eyes stop me from finishing the sentence.

I'm about to give Diane a hug, more for me than for her, when I feel a tap on my shoulder. "I tell you no room to sit, but room to stand," the conductor says, wiping his sweaty head with a rag. I look up into the faces crammed against the windows of the bus. If half the country's population is wandering the depot, the other half is crammed into the bus. I don't know if can handle standing for six hours, my face in somebody's armpit.

"The problem is, sir, my friend here doesn't feel well, and I don't think she can stand for six hours." He regards her with great compassion. "No problem," he says with a big smile. "She have my seat. *You* stand. Come."

I put both my hands on both of her shoulders. This is serious. "Can you make it? It isn't going to be pretty." The answer is crystal clear in her eyes. She would rather lick the ground of this depot than miss this bus. "Vee go."

We step aboard and find ourselves already among passengers. The Big Cheese pushes in behind me. In order to accommodate him, I have to step carefully up between four Malawians cramped with their bags on the stairs. My spot for the next six hours, it seems, will be perching precariously at the top of the stairs.

I am squished between a seat supposed to hold two passengers, but harboring three, and the first seat to my right harboring what seems to be everybody's luggage that *isn't* piled on the passengers' laps, in the aisles, or making up the enormous pyramid on the roof of the bus. One sharp turn and I am going to be squashed beneath this mountain of luggage. In front of the luggage is a box of thick glass protecting the driver. The smell from the sweltering bodies, people's food packed for the trip, and babies' soiled diapers is made bearable only by the hope that I won't have to spend the rest of my life in that spot. Fortunately for Diane, her seat, compassionately offered by the Big Cheese, is the single one right at the left-front.

I turn my head to look behind me and cannot believe what I see. Bus regulation, printed on a dilapidated plaque above the stairs, states that the bus is made to hold sixty-five passengers seated and twenty-five standing. There are easily a hundred seated and at least forty standing. If this bus crashes, like so many buses do across Africa, many might *not* actually die because there are so many bodies cushioning each other. I begin praying that this public bus, my first in Africa, will be an exception to all the buses I've seen passing us at the speed of sound on the tens of thousands of miles I've traveled across Africa. I'm not even going to think about the dozens of bus carcasses I've seen lining African highways and byways.

A half hour out of Lilongwe, I look at Diane to see if her face is as taut with fear as mine feels. Somehow, she is asleep. She clutches her bag to her chest, her head banging gently against the window. Blessedly for her, she doesn't have to see the death we are avoiding every mile we travel down the anorexic byway. I look through the glass enclosing the driver. The speedometer vibrates angrily, buried below the red, which begins at 130 kph (78 mph, give or take). The speed limit is 80 kph but, considering Malawi's byway obstacles, it should be around 40 kph.

We hurtle past endless processions of cavorting children, ladies balancing huge, plastic water jugs on their heads, and men sitting bravely on the edge of the byway. Pigs, cows, dogs, chickens, goats, and bicycles laden down with anything from eggs to piles of wood taunt Fate by using the edge of and crossing the road without trepidation. The only thing that keeps them from becoming roadkill is the driver laying on his horn like a rancorous god offended by their lack of respect. Even the potholes dotting the age-old tarmac like landmines do nothing to dissuade the driver from trying to break the land-speed record.

Four hours later, after endless bumps and bruises and having become a master of human/luggage Tetris (and despised by everyone on the bus, including myself), I manage to find a seat. Being the person at the front of the aisle apparently has no benefit excluding one: you get to learn an unequivocal, universal truth. The concept of letting people off before one gets on the bus, regardless of how many people are already on the bus, hasn't yet evolved in this country.

It is made increasingly interesting when there is standing room only and people are trying to get off with their luggage. I try to help one woman, her arms bulging with bigger biceps than mine, with her bag. I can feel the old hernia acting up as soon as I get the bag in my hands. The suitcase is tiny but is certainly packed with lead or maybe meteorites. It sinks in my arms and I can't quite get it over the head of the man next to me. She decides I'm too much of a wimp to help her, so she shoves me out of the way and grabs her bag from me. She then proceeds to knock embarking people over in a mad scramble down the stairs and out the door.

Although I struggle, amazingly, Diane has no episodes. She spends most of the time slumped unconsciously over her bag, missing all the fun. I'm happy for her that in five and a half hours, she will retain no stress or trauma from this trip. I, on the other hand, will need a vacation from Earth for a couple of months. The idea that I will have to spend yet *another* couple of hours on *another* bus is complete anathema to my being.

"How you doing?" I ask Diane as we stand in Mzuzu's relatively deserted bus station.

"Fine. Ahm happy I don't need to diarrhea or throw up," she says. "My drug for anti-diarrhea verk guut."

Guut girl, I think. *It's the little things in life*. "Let me see if we can find our bus to Nkhata Bay. I hope it hasn't left—"

"Ah need a toilet."

I take her from one end of the depot to the other until we find a toilet. "Please don't leave here until I get back," I say to her. She nods and bolts for the toilet. I ask the nearly comatose man guarding the toilets to please watch her if she comes out before I get back. I promise him some extra kwacha if he does.

I haggle for ten minutes with a Matatu driver. (Matatu translates to "three more" in Swahili. It actually means that Matatu drivers can *always* fit three more people into a minivan, even if they can't.) His lowest price is $150 for a trip to Kande Beach. He is all smiles during our negotiation because he knows he's our last chance to get there tonight. A hundred fifty dollars is extortion at best. I tell him I'll think it over.

I return to Diane with the glorious news. "We missed the connecting bus to Nkhata. Our only choices are to take a Matatu for $150, which I don't recommend; or, we can stay here in Mzuzu for the night and get a bus in the morning."

"No," she insists. "Ah just vant to get there. Let's do it!" She's become a traveling Nik*e* commercial. I sigh. As bad as bus drivers can be, Matatu drivers are worse. Much worse. I pay the attendant for keeping watch, and we head toward the Matatus.

My phone rings. I flip it open thinking it might be Nick from the campsite. "My brothaahhh!" reverberates in my ear. I am speechless. "How are you, my brothaaahhh?" Dallas cries into the phone. I look at Diane. *Turn me over; I'm done on this side.* What could possibly be his reason for calling?

"How can I help you, Dallas?" I ask without emotion.

"How are you, my brothaaahhh? Where are you?! Do you need a taxi? Anything?"

How about a teleportation machine? is what I want to say. "No, Dallas. I'm fine. I'll see you next time we're in Lilongwe."

"Okay, my bro…"

I hang up and, seeing my exasperation, Diane smiles. "TIA," she says.

We stride toward the Matatu driver across the depot. Almost there, a bus slides by. "You said Nkhata Bay, Mat?" Diane asks.

I nod at her.

"Dat's it!" she screams triumphantly.

She's right. The side window bears the sign, NKHATA. I could cry from joy. I don't complain that it is only forty-five minutes late in leaving. "Let's go!"

Much to the chagrin of the Matatu driver, we run after the bus. Fortunately, the exit gate is closed. We reach the doors of the bus as the gate begins screeching open. I look up through the glass of the bus doors. There is breathing room only. There is no way we are going to fit. I rap at the glass anyway. *Desperate times...*

A mortician-faced man spins at the glass to see who would dare bang on the glass of his bus. When he sees us looking pleadingly up at him, his face cracks into a huge smile. He demands the driver open the doors. He beams at us.

"Kande Beach?" I beg.

"You want to go to Kande Beach?"

Diane and I nod in unison.

"Yes! Yes! We go there. Come!" He's more excited than we are. He turns, yells, and gesticulates wildly at the people behind him in the depths of the bus. The bodies squish, push, and heave, miraculously creating space on the stairwell.

As we climb up, a local tries to clamber aboard, riding our wake. The conductor screams ferociously at him. The man grabs onto the railings just inside the bus but can't quite get onto the stairwell. The gate in front of the bus opens. The driver drops into gear and begins rolling the bus through the gate.

The conductor places a hand in the middle of the local's chest and shoves. The local holds on like a barnacle. The conductor screams louder and lifts his foot, aiming it at the local's chest. I want to yell "Please let go!", but the local is smart enough not to deal with the physical and emotional indignity of taking a boot to the head. He lets go and falls back from the entrance, and the driver slams the doors shut. The conductor looks at us triumphantly. "That's seven hundred twenty kwacha for you both!"

As we pull out of Mzuzu city limits, two Malawian women make room for Diane on the stairs. I stand crunched next to the conductor *on* the windshield. I'm not any more thrilled being on the windshield than I was being the first in the aisle on the last bus. At least, I figure, I'll be the first to die if we crash.

The first hour goes by rather swiftly. I am mesmerized by the road ten feet beneath my eyes. It twists and winds up and over the mountains to get to the major byway that runs parallel to Lake Malawi. The road provides the feeling of being on a roller coaster. Thankfully, there are very few vehicles on the road. Most travelers know that the majority of accidents in Africa occur at night. Most of those are probably caused by bus drivers like this one.

Halfway to Kande, we come up behind another bus. It is committing the greatest byway sin: it is not moving as quickly as we are. Our driver decides the best motivator is to ride the back of his bus. If I reached my hand through the windshield, I'd be tickling its bumper.

Our leading adversary has obvious ego issues. Not only does he not want us to pass, but he also decides to play the game of jamming on his brakes to try and make us rear-end him. Our driver is far too savvy for this amateur move. He escalates by provoking this move and then trying to shoot around the braking bus. For the fiftieth time this day, I want to cry.

Eventually the driver in front of us seems to tire. He flicks on his right turn signal. In much of Africa, this means it is okay to pass. Our driver, perhaps knowing this is another trick, doesn't take the bait. His reluctance saves our lives. A truck whizzes by. I have a brain fart trying to process what just happened. My brain searches for comprehension. It finds it: that Absolute F–ker just tried to kill us!

I jerk my head to our driver, who leans over the wheel with a ruthless determination. I am ready to offer my services of jumping the homicidal maniac in the other bus when we pull alongside him. We hit a straightaway. Our captain guns it. I ready myself to deliver a doublehanded bird-flip and a mental spear of death for the other driver. As we pull alongside of the other bus, however, reason takes over.

Aside from the fact that our bus driver was provoking him, the other driver has a bus filled with passengers as well. Flipping him off and wishing him disaster may very well lead to further escalation and disaster for everyone. Africa has more than its share of hotheadedness. Although I feel justified, I don't want to add to it. We jet past the other bus. I decide a very mean grimace will suffice. The other driver doesn't even look over at us. *TIA, Mat. TIA,* I think as we take the lead.

At Chinteche, several miles still from the Kande Beach drop-off, a handsome twenty-something Malawian fellow clambers aboard. He smiles his perfect white smile at me. "Hi!" he says cheerfully. Needless to say, I'm not so cheerful. "Hi" is all I can muster.

Seeing he's getting nothing from me, he looks down at Diane. "Hi! I'm Andy," he says and puts out his hand to her. She grins. I can see she is already smitten. "Where are you from?"

"Ahm Sviss," she coos.

"Where are you going?" he grins back.

"Kande Beach."

"Me, too! I'm from Kande. My village is there ."

Kande Andy?

"Oh, how nice," she says. "Maybe you show us vere to go."

He smiles even wider. He nods at me, and I nod back at him, skeptical but not unfriendly.

We get to the Kande bus stop. Andy heads off into the darkness of a road, expecting us to follow him. Diane is hot on his heels. I stop her, and then I call to him. "Sorry, my friend," I say. "I don't mean to sound cynical or rude, but we don't know you. You could have a bunch of friends waiting for us."

My statement shocks him. "No! No! No! We don't do that here! We are all friends here. You will see. I am tour guide for the village. I will take you to the resort tonight. Tomorrow you will come with me to the village! You will see! We are all friends here!"

I nod at him. It *is* the friendliest country in Africa, and we could use someone to show us the rest of the way. As we fall in behind him, I think, *The odds are slim, but I'm hoping he's not related to Ming.*

"How far is it to camp?" queries Diane. She is quite obviously hurting since she hasn't eaten all day and the road is ankle-deep sand.

"It's only three kilometers," he says energetically. We both almost fall over. Diane whimpers.

"Everything okay?" asks Andy good-naturedly.

I know Diane is thinking what I'm thinking. *No, Kande Andy, everything is not okay. Three kilometers might as well be Mars.*

He sees our pain. "Here, let me help you." He takes Diane's bag from her and smiles compassionately at us. "Come. We will be there before you know it." Diane smiles widely back at him. It's going to be alright.

As we walk, Andy asks lots of questions. He shows great interest in Diane, so I fall back behind them. I want him to occupy her, so I don't mention I am the tour leader on our truck. He would feel obligated to entertain me as my passengers are a part of his livelihood. Andy's chief is the one who allowed the resort to be built on the village's land. This benefits all members of the village, like Kande Andy, when the overland trucks roll in.

Kande Andy regales all the wonderful things that Diane will see the next day. She loses herself in this young man and their chemistry. She is obviously invigorated by the thought of spending the next day with him. After her brutal day that began sixteen hours before, I'm happy that her day is ending like this.

It takes me about a kilometer before I start thanking whatever powers that be for Andy. The sandy road branches into a thousand different forks. If I had had to get us to the resort from the bus stop, we may have ended up back in Lilongwe.

It is around ten o' clock when we arrive at the gates of Kande Beach Resort. We can hear the soft lapping of the waves on the beach. Andy shakes my hand and says to Diane he will be there at ten o' clock to pick her up the next morning. He disappears into the darkness like a phantom. Her beaming face as she watches him dematerialize is the only evidence that he actually existed.

We step through the gate. Our truck is parked like a welcome mirage not a hundred yards from us. In the dim lighting of lamps everywhere, it looks like paradise. "Ah can't believe vee make it," Diane says, exhaustedly. We walk to the truck and drop our bags. Mwai, our cook, greets us with a warm grin. "Dinner is ready when you are ready." I could hug him.

"How was your trip?" everybody asks as they find us devouring our dinner. Diane and I shake our heads, too exhausted to explain. "We'll tell you about it tomorrow," I murmur. It is obvious to them that recanting our story might kill us.

After finishing dinner, I can barely stand from the stool. Diane smiles at me. "Tank you, tank you, Mat. Ah so happy you get us here."

I smile tiredly back at her. "You did good, kid. Make sure you thank Kande Andy tomorrow. We wouldn't be here if it weren't for him."

She chuckles. "I vill be happy to."

I say goodnight to her and head for bed.

I'm too tired for a shower but, after spending the whole day cramped between sweaty armpits and dirty luggage, I know that skipping it might be dangerous. I almost fall asleep in the shower. I finally make it to bed. I lay back and my eyelids immediately begin to close. The phone rings. For some reason I think it might be my parents, so I pick up the phone. "Hello?" I hear only voices and drum-based music in the background. "Hello?" I ask again.

"My brothaaahhh!"

I flip the phone closed. *TIA, Mat. TIA...*

THE CALL OF THE AFRICAN WILD

The particular scream I hear as we are putting up our tents at Chitimba Overland Resort, Malawi, is easily recognized by experienced guides. It is a sound made by just about any tourist any place in Africa. It is a shocked, shrill, high-pitched banshee-call, usually followed by an expletive or an expression of complete revolted incredulousness. It is one of my favorites.

It means that some African creature has, either willingly or unwillingly, made its presence known to those unfortunate enough *not* to have seen it before. I request at the beginning of every trip, "Please, guys, if you ever encounter any kind of beastie anywhere, yell for me and I promise I will come running to see what you have found or what has found you!" Thus, with my passengers, the scream and expletive is inevitably followed by "Mat! Mat! Come quick!"

"Ahhhhhh! What the f–k is *that* thing?" Jen shrieks from across the campsite. I'm already running as I hear her husband, Dev's, "F–k if I know! It's disgusting!", and then the much anticipated, "Mat! Mat! Come quick!"

I race around the bar area and then over to Jen and Dev's tent. Staring in horrified fascination at something on the ground, they both point at the creature as if I would miss it. It is pretty much unmissable.

"Awesome!" I yell, unable to contain my enthusiasm. I drop down to a knee to admire the impressive, uninvited entity. It is about four inches long and an inch wide with a predominantly golden body striped black and brown down its thorax and abdomen; it has big black eyes and huge jaws. It moves with alarming speed, low to the ground as if on a mission, perhaps, to eat your toes if it were so inclined. It stops, digs ferociously in the sand and then moves to another excavation site like a tiny, six-legged machine in overdrive.

"It's my first sand cricket!" I add as if I just found the Loch Ness Monster. They are summarily unimpressed as evidenced by the scowls of disgust writ upon their faces.

"Are you gonna pick it up?" Jen asks with both trepidation and anticipation.

"Uh, no," I answer. "If you look closely at its mandibles, you can see that they are made for carving. They are known to be primarily carnivorous and deliver an extremely painful bite."

Jen involuntarily steps back and grabs Dev's arm. "It's… It's…," she searches for the perfect word, "It's…monstrous!" she exclaims. "Will it dig under the tent and get in there with us?"

I snicker. That would definitely be worth the price of admission.

"No, Jen, it is not going to dig under your tent and get in there with you. It is totally harmless and will only bite you if you pick it up or harass it. It is usually nocturnal, wandering around at night looking for prey. After feeding, it digs burrows in which to hide during the day. You probably disturbed him putting up the tent on his burrow."

"*We* disturbed *him?*" she cries. "I think I'm gonna be sick…"

A flutter sounds above our heads to the right, and a mad chirping commences. I look up and a dark-capped bulbul calls angrily at us from its perch not two yards from us. "Oh, look guys! A dark-capped bulbul!"

They look up at the boisterous bird as if their quota for creepy creatures has been filled for the day. "It's a little crazy, isn't it?" Dev asks skeptically.

I laugh. "It is, isn't it? And close! No wild bird usually comes this close unless protecting a nest." The bulbul chirps and jumps up and down on the branch like it is hopped up on crystal meth.

We look back down at the cricket. It wanders about my feet looking for softer sand within which to dig his burrow. "Great find, guys," I state appreciatively. "Thanks for calling me over."

I back up so as not to step on the cricket. "So what are your plans for the day?" I ask to take their minds off the creature at their feet. They step back to the tent to zip it in case the marauding insect decides to get in their domicile. Jen puts her hands on her hips, "I think the beach sounds good, but Dev wants to—" She doesn't get a chance to finish her sentence.

In a flurry of feathers, the bulbul swoops down and grabs the cricket in its beak. Jen screams for a second time. The bird stands there with the cricket as if to show us how stupid we were for not eating it ourselves. Satisfied with its ego-maniacal display, the bird then launches itself up onto the same branch with the wriggling insect.

Jen fixates her eyes full on me. "Mat! Mat...!" she shrieks. "DO SOMETHING!"

Dev and I look at her as shocked by her outburst as by the bird's audacity.

"What should I do?" I laugh.

"I don't know! *SOMETHING!* It's got the cricket!" she cries as if it was her pet poodle being carried away by an eagle.

"Two seconds ago you were saying it was monstrous! Now you want me to save it?"

The bird flies away with the cricket, leaving us to watch it helplessly.

Dev and I look at Jen to see if she is going to be alright. She doesn't look like she's going to be alright. Dev puts an arm around her. "You gonna be alright, Hon?" he asks condescendingly.

She pushes him away. "I don't know! It just wasn't supposed to happen like that," Jen says despairingly, her head falling into her hands. Dev and I raise our eyebrows at one another.

I decide I should try and lessen the blow. "Well, I don't know if this will make you feel better, but think of it this way. There's no doubt the Circle of Life can be a traumatic thing, but you did mention that you wanted to see a kill while you were here in Africa. You just got to see your first kill."

HAMBURGER FOR RENT

Zanzibar has always sounded like the most exotic place in the world to me. It is an island paradise off the coast of Dar es Salaam, Tanzania. To get to Zanzibar, one must take a ferry or fly in. Although officially Tanzania, Zanzibar would like to have its independence back since it joined Tanzania in 1964. (Tanzania is the combining of the names *Tanganyika,* or mainland Tanzania, and Zanzibar.) When you arrive in Zanzibar, you must even present your passport and clear customs.

Steeped in history, going all the way back to long before the death of Christ and the rise of Islam, it is one of Africa's premiere vacation spots. Cloaked in the darkness of its slave trade past and brightened by the promise of sun, fun, Fusion cuisine, and a host of aquatic activities, it is the once-upon-a-time home of David Livingstone, perhaps the greatest influence in conquering the slave trade, and the birthplace of Freddie Mercury of Queen. It is the only place in the world where one can see the remaining Red Colobus monkeys.

It is a place of unimaginable natural beauty and a place suffering the consequences of nearly a million people living on 950 square miles. It is a place with culture so thick, one has to shower it from one's self at the end of the day. The mixture of cultures and peoples from the Arab world, the inner tribes of Africa, and expats from all over the world makes for some of the most striking human beauty one will ever see.

Although Zanzibar's impossibly claustrophobic population suffers from joblessness and an incredibly overtaxed social security system, people are incredibly friendly. Wherever you go in the streets, on the beaches, and in the endless maze of shop-filled back alleys, the Zanzibari citizens are there to welcome you, assist you and, of course, sell you anything and everything. People have found ways of surviving that only a place like Zanzibar could imagine…

It is my first night in Stonetown, Zanzibar. I need a break from people after my first thirty-five days of being an overlanding guide and, thus, want a romantic evening with myself. I want to try local dining, not another tourist restaurant. I walk the streets trying my best to avoid eye contact with the dozens of men lining the streets waiting in the shadows to sell me "Jambo, Jambo Bwana" CDs, t-shirts, paintings, taxi services, drugs, girls, tours, and everything else imaginable.

I think of my experience earlier in the afternoon. A toothless fellow named Abdullah, his skullcap skewed to the side of his head, tried to stop me with a loud "Let me help you, friend!" After a morning of being overwhelmed with similar offers, I responded with a "No, no, let me help *you!*"

He sensed my impatience and frowned. Then he launched into a semi-coherent diatribe on how I should appreciate Zanzibar and its friendly people and understand that it is low season, and this is the only way for Zanzibar to make money. And, if he made a mistake, he is sorry but obviously I am the one making the mistake because I won't stop and give him a chance to sell me whatever it is he might want to sell me. Feeling guilty and uncultured and caught in his co-dependent trap, I chatted with him for ten minutes until he seemed satisfied with my cultural education. In the end, his pride won out. He walked off without trying to sell me anything.

I arrive through a labyrinth of ancient stone walls at a modernized colonial structure known as The Africa House. It is a popular tourist spot for sunset and, after Abdullah earlier, I feel it is especially not the place I should be. I go to the concierge and smile broadly. "Can you point me to a local restaurant, one that has good food and one that you would eat at?"

He smiles back at me. "Where are you from?" he asks with interest.

"I am from the United States," I say, not certain how he will react to that response.

"I looooove Amerrricans!" he shouts. "They are so frrriendly! I knew the minute you asked you wanted local food you are Amerrrican. I knew it! Ha! Ha!"

He shoots around the desk and pumps my hand. "Come!" He nudges me out the door to where another fellow stands in a glittering skullcap of gold and maroon, flowing white shirt, genie-like pants, and a maroon vest that denotes his place as doorman. "Santana will show you to the restaurant! Enjoy, my Amerrrican frrriend!" He waves us off.

Santana immediately removes the skullcap and vest. "I am Santana." He whips out a card and deftly places it in my outstretched hand. "I am a tour guide."

In Zanzibar, at some point or another, everyone is.

I find myself trailing behind him as he winds his way through the maze of streets. In his somewhat comprehensible English, he is already telling me about his ideas of guiding. "Spice tours are good for people, but dere is more, much more to Zanzibar. I take people to weddings and funerals in same day. Imagine that! Same day! You know how hard it is to find dis in same day. People love it! I take people to traditional meal with family. *Dat* is culture! *Dat* is guiding! Yes, they go to Prison Island and see the tortoise. Yes, dey go to House of Wonder and Slave Market! But people must know Zanzibar people!" He emphasizes all this with two hands waving about in front of him.

Obviously not having learned my lesson from Abdullah, I ask ironically, "Does this mean you're coming to dinner with me, Santana?"

He spins around to me with a big grin. "Wonderful! I can eat something! Come!"

He leads me down the main street and pulls up at an inadequately labeled restaurant. He whisks me up the stairs to an outside patio. There are several tables filled with Zanzibari residents. He pulls out a chair at a table with two attractive ladies. They smile seductively at me, more than ready to welcome a stranger. "You want to sit here maybe?" he invites. I recognize immediately that he is testing me. I'm smart enough to understand that in a Muslim-dominated culture where most women walk around with their heads covered at least, that two suggestively-clad ladies in a restaurant are there for one reason and dinner is not it.

I smile and shake my head.

"Ahhhh! You want to sit over here!" He leads me past the hostess who seems to know better than to get involved with the male seat-selection process. We sit under an Ashok tree (A pretty tree that looks like a tired, leafy Christmas tree) at a long table capable of seating eight.

As soon as we sit, a diminutive, bone-thin, scraggly-bearded fellow who definitely hasn't washed this year pulls up the next empty chair at the table and grasps my hand. "My name is Yusef. I like you! You have honest eyes." He reeks of alcohol. I look questioningly at Santana as I believe it is one of his friends or relatives. He frowns at Yusef and says something gruffly to him in Swahili.

Yusef is not to be dissuaded. It is evident that he is going to be joining us for dinner as well. "My friend! How are you? You are Canadian, no? Welcome to Stonetown, my home. You are welcome. *Karibu!*" he shouts, mindless of the scene he is creating. I look around to see if the hostess is watching her patrons being harassed by this obviously drugged-out man of the streets. Her nonchalance conveys the fact that he is a regular here. Santana looks exasperated.

It becomes obvious to me that Yusef is seen by all as tribes used to see their "crazy people" or their "misfits." As long as they aren't hurting anyone, they are accepted. Santana obviously has a lot to share with his newfound American friend. I can see, however, he doesn't want to share it with Yusef sitting there eyeballing us.

I turn to Yusef. "Yusef. Listen. I don't mean to be rude in any way, but Santana, here, and I have some very important business to discuss that is private. I hope you understand."

Yusef looks searchingly into my eyes and nods. "I am going to leave you two because you have honest eyes. I know you think I'm a little crazy, but I'm not crazy. I just quit smoking and that is why I drink now. I'm an alcoholic now because I quit smoking."

I try to process the logic of it. "Maybe you should quit both," I suggest.

"How about you give me two thousand shillings?" he retorts.

I try hard not to laugh. "I'm sorry, Yusef. I can't do that."

He looks like he is about to cry. Santana starts in on him, pleading for him to go away.

"I not eat today. Please, just two thousand for a hamburger. Please. I'm so hungry. It is for me and my friend over there." He points to another rough-looking character, baked out of his mind and barely able to sit upright on the stairs.

I think about the money. It is about $1.75. As a general rule, I will buy food for a person in need who asks for it. I will not just give money, as more often than not it will go to a less than noble destination. I've already broken my charity budget for the trip, and I'm buying dinner for Santana. *Ah hell with it,* I decide. Yusef definitely looks hungry, and I'm too tired to be cynical.

I take out the money. Santana holds his hand in front of it. He says something to Yusef, but Yusef protests. Santana works him some more, and Yusef acquiesces. "I go get the hamburger and bring it back," Yusef slurs. Before I can get an answer to my question of where the hell is he going to get a hamburger without money, he bolts from the restaurant with his lurching pal.

Santana looks at me seriously. "Don't give him the money until he takes a bite."

"What?" I ask, not comprehending.

"He will get the hamburger, show it to you, and den take it back. Den he goes buy drugs. Make sure he takes a bite."

It sounds utterly absurd. "You're telling me that there is some guy down the street who will rent a hamburger for him to show and will then sell it to someone else after he brings it back?"

Santana eyes me like it is obvious. "Dere are many ways to make money here," he states with the wisdom of what I later learn is his twenty-seven years.

A half hour later (and after Santana's rather sad life story of having been orphaned at seven, placed in an orphanage, and then mentored at fifteen by a caring teacher who saw his potential) the dynamic duo of Yusef and his pal return bearing a small package of tinfoil.

Santana instructs him to open it and lay it on the table. Yusef does as he is told. "Eat," Santana instructs Yusef.

Yusef eats a couple of pieces of lettuce and what could be chicken. He then folds it all back up. He stuffs it in his pocket and holds out his hand for the money. Astounded, I give him the money. If he's willing to go through all this trouble, I feel like he deserves it.

Yusef jumps up from the table. "Thank you, my friend! God bless you!" Yusef and his pal then disappear like Pigpen ninjas into the night with their money. Santana shakes his youthful head and sighs.

After dinner, Santana thanks me for sharing my guiding experiences with him, and I thank him for sharing his with me. We part company with an African handshake and express our hope to see one another when I return.

"You know where to find me. Call me when you return. I take your people around," he says hopefully. "Funeral *and* wedding in same day."

I walk back toward the hotel feeling good to have stepped out of my comfort zone and spending time with locals. *Renting a hamburger*, I think. It makes me sad that such a thing is possible. It also makes me feel there are small triumphs in the struggle so many face in Africa. Above all, it makes me realize I still have a lot to learn about this place I am in love with.

CHAPTER THREE

LIZARD LOVES

THE DREAM DRAGON

The Oryx stand in the red grass of Big Hoek, a hundred yards in front of the Land Rover. They eye us nervously as we putter up the road toward them. We have just taken an untold number of photos of eland (Africa's largest antelope species), "Chippy," our second largest white rhino on the reserve (who would later, tragically, be poached for his horn in 2010); and a herd of Burchell's zebra and their constant companions, a small herd of black wildebeests.

The Oryx, however, were our original quarry and a great prize as they are not commonly seen on the reserve. With the sun behind us, my favorite of the antelope species, characterized by their light gray coats, black face masks, white underbellies, and huge and straight horns are going to make an awesome photo for the guests if I can get a little closer. I missile-lock on them; I need to judge the comfort zone between us and them perfectly so they do not flee as we approach.

I am so intent on them that I actually jump in my seat when Saraya, traveling with her husband, Jack, shrieks, "There's a huge lizard back there in the grass!"

Well, I feel it then: the *dream emotion*. It is that tingling sensation one gets when one realizes something great and momentous is about to occur, like the fulfilling of a dream. It could be only one thing out here in the middle of Big Hoek. It has to be a monitor lizard. I jam on the brakes. Ever since I could say Komodo dragon, I've had the dream of catching one of these lizards.

I look in the side mirror and see the lizard's four-foot body just off the road in the red grass. It is a medium-size one, as they can be well over six feet long. Its bluish and yellow scales shine like a light-house beacon, guiding me back to my dream of yesteryear. I grind the Land Rover into reverse and gun it backward.

I am a good five yards from the lizard when I break hard. Nobody even has a chance to curse me for the abrupt stop before I sweep open my door. I leap out of the Landie and hit the ground running. In his tiny reptilian brain, it takes the lizard a second to realize his sitting motionless in the grass isn't going to work as his first line of defense.

He wisely bolts for it, pushing through the knee-high grass straight for the eland, zebra, and black wildebeest. I race after him, the smile on my face getting bigger by the step. My once-hurting knees, anesthetized by the fact I'm pumping it to catch a dream, cut through the red grass like a scythe.

Now, I knew this lizard would be fast. What I didn't reckon on is its ability to outrun me over the first ten yards. Since he got the jump on me at five yards, he does a damn good job of not allowing me to close that gap. On top of his speed, he also has the added ben-efit of being three inches off the ground (very low center of gravity) and having a tail almost twice as long as his body. This allows him to zigzag all over the show like he is on alternating rubber bands. I start to feel like Rocky trying to catch the chicken.

As we dart across the field, I can see that being three inches at the shoulders is not as helpful as I thought when running through grass a foot and a half high. Bless the powers that be that made me a biped with legs taller than red grass. At thirty yards out, I close the gap between us and am just beyond his tail.

It then occurs to me that my efforts have just begun. I know he isn't going to stop until he finds himself a hole in which to hide. This means I'll have to grab him out here in the open. Grabbing him promises the possibility of serious biting, definite scratching, and tail-lashing that is the equivalent of a small whip.

Monitors have serious teeth and tend to hold on like Bull Terriers. If they have been feeding on carrion, there is the possibility of septicemia. Their claws are capable of ripping through a cement-like termite mound (wherein they lay their eggs and allow the mound to incubate them). As for the tail, one of our field guides actually had his pants ripped by the lashing of a monitor's tail. All this means that if I am going to grab him, I have to grab him behind the head on my first attempt. The question arises then: how do you grab a writhing miniature dragon exactly in the right place while running through a field at top speed? My answer is less than elegant to say the least.

My right hand lands just in front of his back legs where his tail meets his body. He neatly meets my left forearm (heading for his neck to do what my right hand had failed to do) with his jaws wide open. He clamps firmly down on my (thankfully) long-sleeved shirt. He grasps my right arm with his two back legs, digging the nastily-curved claws into my inner bicep and outer tricep. He follows that up with repeated attempts to slap me senseless with his incredibly powerful tail.

Tangled together with talons, teeth, and tail, I feel I may have bitten off more than he can chew. Although I definitely have the weight and arguably the intelligence advantage, he definitely has the weapon advantage. I struggle to pull my left arm out of his mouth and get a hold under his neck. For a good three minutes, we wrestle like that in the grass under the curious eyes of the zebra, wildebeests, and eland.

The strength in his mouth, digits, and tail astounds me. With his claws and tail wrapped around my arm, I can barely move it. My

Ulovane work shirt is blessedly thick, or I would certainly be nursing some serious stitches. I manage to work my left hand to the base of his long throat. Using my right knee, I manage to remove his left leg from my inner right arm. My coup de grace is moving my right hand over the base of his tail, thus grabbing it so his claws can't grab me and tail can't whip me in the head anymore.

As soon as I get this position, the lizard goes completely limp. In other words, he enacts *thanatosis,* or plays dead. This, and crapping all over you with the most foul-smelling poop one has ever smelled, are the last means of defense most reptiles employ when all else fails. Fortunately, he decides just to limp out.

I arise from the grass, beaming. I look across the plain and am rather shocked to see how far I have traveled in hot pursuit. The antelope and zebra, now quite close, hurrumph at my proximity to them. Having not moved, they may have been just as entertained as my guests.

I make the long trek back to the Land Rover where everyone is laughing and clapping. I am on top of the world. I have bagged the dream dragon. When I get there, the cameras are whirring. I can't stop smiling. The Monitor sticks out his purple–blue, forked tongue and gives us all a smell. He is a vision of every herpetophobe's worst nightmare. He is absolutely *beautiful.*

"Isn't he beautiful?" I ask, holding it like it is my firstborn. Saraya and Dana answer me with simple facial expressions, like they are afraid I might hand the lizard to them. If I did that, there is no doubt they would spontaneously combust. Dana's husband, Baxter, says it best: "Well, Mat, we're sure it is to *you.*"

When I lay the Monitor in the grass, I feel like I have accomplished something wonderful. I watch him with a combination of awe and joy. He sits there for a second, hardly believing that he has a chance at freedom. If he could think, I'm sure he would be thinking,

Thanatosis. Works every time. He bolts from us once again, blazing yet another trail through the red grass.

I turn to my passengers who are bemused. I sigh and smile broadly. "Thank you, guys. You have joined me in living a dream." They all think I'm missing a few marbles. Truth is, all dreamers have to be in some shape or form.

HAVE A BITE

Dale, a thirty-three-year-old, burly New Zealander with a bushy beard is married to a lovely woman, Jane. She constantly shakes her head in consternation and admiration at his antics. He is a carpenter and the proverbial tough guy who likes his rugby, beer, and his p-nis.

For our immensely popular talent show, which I've institution-alized for every three-week trip, Dale decided to do "Naked Air Guitar" as his first act. He placed first in the competition with his AC/DC solo number covered only by an air mattress. He ended this engrossing act by flipping open the mattress by mistake. He flashed half the audience, which definitely lost him a couple votes— or earned him some.

Having placed in the top three, he then had to do a second act to win the show over the second- and third-place contestants. He fol-lowed up with "Penis Puppetry" and his version of "Wristwatch." It's possible that because he didn't do "Helicopter" or "Belt," he didn't win the talent show.

With the same intrepid attitude, our not-shy New Zealander finds himself at the Snake Park in Swakopmund, Namibia, staring at my favorite African creature, the Namaqua chameleon. Stuart, the man who owns and runs the Reptile House and a Namibian hero for the preservation of its creatures, pulls one of the large-headed, eight-inch beasties from the cage. It opens its mouth with its brilliant orange–yellow inside in a defensive display.

"Anyone want to try a bite?" Stuart asks us cordially. We're not quite sure what he means. He holds up the lizard. "Anyone want to feel what it is like to be bitten by him?"

I do, of course. For his size, the chameleon has a massive head, and I am curious to find how hard it bites. I walk over, much to the consternation of my passengers, and offer it my hand. "No, no," Stuart admonishes. "You have to give it a finger; if it decides to pull away from you, it will tear the loose skin."

Sound advice. I offer it the side of my little finger.

The chameleon doesn't hesitate to bite me. It clamps down on my finger with very impressive force. Having been bitten a couple hundred times by any number of reptiles, I am not surprised by the strength in its jaws. After all, it has to be able to crush insects' exoskeletons to get the prey down its throat. I hold my hand there for three seconds without moving. He finally decides he's proved his point and releases me. I admire the indentations on my finger. Tiny pinpricks of blood mark where his teeth broke the skin. I am unharmed and proud to have received a bite from my favorite African animal.

Dale squints at me. I can see the testosterone sloshing behind his eyes conveying, *If he can do it, so can I.* Jane shakes her head in my peripheral vision. She knows exactly what he is thinking and how these things turn out with her husband. Ten seconds go by before his testosterone sways the day.

"Did it hurt?" he asks.

I shake my head. "It only feels like a pinch. You're a tough guy. You won't even feel it," I say.

He laughs and steadies his hand in front of the hapless lizard. The creature's beady eyes focus on me and Dale simultaneously, trying to decide which one of us is still the threat.

Dale inches his finger toward the lizard's awaiting jaws. The lizard focuses both its bulbous eyes on the digit; it needs to go binocular (both eyes forward) to judge distance. Just as Stuart and I open our mouths to warn Dale not to jerk away, the lizard jerks forward. It clamps on Dale's finger like it is lunch.

"Ahhh!" Dale shrieks like a three-year-old girl. He jerks his hand up and down. The poor lizard hangs on like a bulldog chomping a swinging tire. It is obviously torn between flying several yards to an uncertain fate or having his neck broken from Dale's vigorous shaking. After a couple seconds, it decides on the former. It takes to space like a scaly meteorite. He bounces off the side of his cage and lands with a thump on the soft sand of his terrarium.

My hands on my head and my eyes wide with horror, I yell, "What have you done?"

Dale is visibly distraught. "I'm sorry! I'm sorry, but he got me! He got me good! I didn't expect it to be so strong! How would we have gotten him off?"

I check the chameleon for signs of life. It looks up at us with what looks like great disdain and marches off to his little perch to nurse what must be more than one bruise.

Dale rubs his hand sheepishly.

Stuart breaks into a laugh. "I forgot to tell you not to move."

"F–k that," Dale growls. "That's the last time I offer my hand to anything for biting."

"Well," I say, "it could have been worse."

"How's that exactly?"

I smile. "You could've offered it your wristwatch."

A REPTILE DYSFUNCTION

I became a guide as much because I love to educate and share the beauties of Nature with others as I love Nature itself. There is almost nothing grander in a day than showing people an animal or plant they didn't know existed and seeing how that organism helps them appreciate and see the world in a different, even magical way.

The process of doing this, however, is unpredictable at best, and possibly foolish or fatal at worst. Obviously, the worst is to be avoided at all costs. It doesn't do anyone any good to try and catch an animal to share its beauty with your clients and it *kills* you. That is defeating the purpose.

Andy, my fellow guide from Leeuwenbosch Lodge, drives us on the road, cutting a serpentine swath through Big Hoek. We are heading to visit one of my favorite denizens of the reserve, Big O. Big O is a scorpion from the genus Opistophthalmus who has been living under the same rock for the better part of a year. Sitting in the back of the Land Rover is a very nice, young couple: Hans, a German, and Marta, an Irishwoman. Behind them are Andy's father, uncle, and their good friend, just in from Stellenbosch (wine country) and on their BMW road bikes. It is a beautiful day, and I am very excited to be out on the reserve.

We have already just missed killing several Leopard tortoises (one of the Little Five) making their mad dashes out of the red grass and across the dirt roads of the reserve. I start babbling about the importance of having grasses like red grass on one's reserve when Andy jams on the brakes. "There's a huge cobra, Mat. Go catch it!"

Before I can ask the obvious "Why don't *you* go catch it?", I instinctively leap up from my seat, adrenalized with my usual herpetological passion. The Cape Cobra slithering across the road in front of us is indeed an enormous one. Bright yellow with black, brown, and orange flecks on its six-foot body, it is an absolutely perfect specimen. Without even opening the door, I launch myself out of the vehicle, Andy on my heels.

I have caught venomous snakes before and am well aware of the danger. I had asked Dr. Bill Branch, a world-renowned zoologist working in Port Elizabeth, if there were any snakes in Africa that he would rather lose a limb to than allow a possible envenomation to occur if there was no help nearby. He answered without hesitation or equivocation: "Yes. The Black Mamba and the Cape Cobra."

As I race after the snake in the grass, I keep this in mind.

The snake, unwilling to cooperate with our game of show and tell, disappears into the waving grasses. I know it is going to be difficult to see it in the grass as its coloration blends in perfectly there. I certainly don't want to step on it. I do, however, want it to rear up and present its hood for a photo opportunity. Both Andy and I walk very slowly through the grass, scrutinizing the ground in front of us.

"Do you see it?" Andy asks.

I am disappointed that I don't. "Sh-t...no," I respond dejectedly. They can move so quickly that it's possible the thing is already a good twenty yards from us in any direction.

"That was a Cape Cobra, Dad. The most venomous snake on the reserve, maybe in all of Africa!" Andy says.

I cast one last look around me and shrug it off. This is the first one I've seen in seven months. The fact that the Leopard tortoises are out means it is getting warmer. I will see more cobras soon. I look at the Landie now, a good thirty yards from me, and take a step back toward it.

A sibilant hiss stops me cold. I look down to see the cobra's length streaming not four inches from my foot. It slithers by me, around a little bush, and shoots straight as an arrow into an aardvark hole three yards from me. I am dumbfounded. I just missed stepping on the thing's head. I stand there for a second and try not to imagine what would have happened if I had stepped on the poor creature. *Hello...Dr. Branch? I thought you should know as I expel my last breath, you were right on about the Cape Cobra.* I vow this is the last time I decide to chase after a venomous snake where I cannot see it. *Much better to be handling scorpions,* I think as I get back in the Landie.

Twenty minutes later, we are cruising down Old Bay Road and I signal Andy to stop. We have reached Big O's rock. He has been in hibernation for a few months and, as it is warming up, may very well be ready to join us for a round of show and tell. He is one of the few species here that I will pick up to show the guests. His sting hurts like hell, but his venom is about as toxic as a wasp sting. The scorpions with the tiny claws and huge stinger, like the Granulated thick-tailed scorpions, are the ones you don't pick up. Because he has huge claws that he uses to catch his prey and defend himself, Big O very rarely will use his stinger. That being said, I've been pinched by Big O. It hurts like hell, too.

I look under Big O's rock with our guests watching, but Big O is still deep in his hole. I try coaxing him out with a blade of grass, which he usually takes hold of with a kung-fu grip. Then I pull him out and pick him up by the end of his tail, where I can control his telson (stinger). Today, he isn't taking, and I don't want to bother him more than I already have; so I close the rock back down over his hole.

I turn to another rock adjacent to Big O's. It usually has nothing under it, but it's always the rock you don't try that has the critter. On my knees, I scoot over and lift the rock. Sure enough, a Cape Skink (a pretty, whitish, no-necked, smooth-skinned lizard) cocks his head to the side to see who just pulled the roof off his hideaway.

My hand shoots down to catch him, but he is too quick. He runs under some miniature succulents next to my knee. My other hand slinks down and gently presses him under the little plants so I can grab him a little more easily. He squiggles to just under my knee, so I move my knee to the left and try to grab him. I miss. He takes this opportunity to run back along my leg and up my pant leg. I fall backward onto my butt cheeks and press him gently against my shin so he doesn't get up any higher.

"What's happening?" Andy asks. Everyone is watching intently.

"The little dude ran up my pant leg!" I laugh.

"Do you need some help?"

"I got him." I say this as casually as possible, as if this sort of thing happens all the time.

I try and work him downward, but the skink is having none of it. He wriggles up a little further, taking advantage of the fact that I don't want to squish him. His claws dig into my skin. I start giggling, as much from how much it tickles as how silly this must look from the guests' point of view.

My pant intruder wiggles a little higher to just below my knee. I try and reach up my pants to get him, and all I can feel is his tail. I don't want to grab him by his tail as he might autotomize (self-mutilate by dropping his tail), which will make it difficult for him to find a mate in the future. (Most females of most lizard species prefer unmarred mates.) My pant leg openings are too tight to reach up any further. This is getting *ridiculous*.

I laugh even harder when Andy appears at my side, his hand extended like an overzealous proctologist.

"Dude, let me try," he offers. He sticks his hand up my pant leg without permission as I hold onto the skink's upper body. "I can only grab his tail. I don't want him to lose it."

Such good, conscientious guides we are.

A look of serious concentration appears on Andy's face. He shoves both hands up my pant leg. By now, tears stream down my face from the laughter.

"Oh, screw it!" I yell. I smack Andy's hands to get him to retreat. Andy starts laughing and crying as hard as I am. He rolls backward on his butt. I jump to my feet and lose hold of the lizard. It shoots up my inner thigh and disappears.

I look down at my crotch with my arms up in the air. *Is that a Cape Skink in your pants, or are you just happy to see me?* runs through my head.

"Where'd it go?" Andy chokes through the laughter.

I shake my head, incredulous. "I don't know! It's gone!" The men are cackling in the Landie, but I hear nothing from Hans and Marta.

Somebody needs to be the voice of reason in the midst of this ridiculousness. Marta decides to be that voice. "If, um, you need, um, to take off your pahnts, Maht, I can, um, turn away," she calls to me. That kills me. If lack of professionalism was an animal, this would be a blue whale.

I hold my side, cramped from laughing, and search my groin area. I find the skink moving between my cell phone in my left pocket and the pant itself. I'm going to *have to* take off my pants. I undo my belt, my button, and my zipper. The animal scuttles left, around toward my left butt cheek. I block him and peel back my pants.

The cheeky bugger hangs from my pocket. He cocks his head at me with what definitely looks like a smile. *Really funny, you little knucklehead.* I slowly lower my hand down to grab him. He takes that as his cue to shoot down my thigh. He races down behind my knee, my calf, out my cuff, across my boot, and back under the rock.

Excluding Hans and Marta, everyone is still laughing. It takes Andy and me a good two minutes to pull ourselves together.

"That was the funniest thing I've ever seen!" Andy exclaims.

"It's a damn good thing I don't get embarrassed," I add, embarrassed. I'm praying nobody got it on film. Andy and I walk back to the vehicle still chuckling.

"Are you alright?" Marta asks me seriously.

I look at her quizzically. "Oh, yeah. They're harmless," I say.

Marta and Hans exchange confused looks. "I thought you said scorpions could hurt you," Hans says.

It's my turn to be confused. "Most scorpions are harmless. The one I was going to show you, the Opistophthalmus, will hurt if it stings you, but it isn't dangerous," I answer.

"Did it sting you, then?" Hans asks, mystified.

"The scorpion?" I ask, still confused. "No, he didn't want to come out of his hole."

Hans and Marta look at each and then back at me, utterly bewildered. Marta eyes me almost angrily and, with her thick Irish brogue, which is somehow even funnier, she asks, "So, what the hell were ya fushin' out of your pahnts, Maht?"

I'm laughing again thinking how they must have seen it. "The thing that ran up my leg was a lizard called a skink; it wasn't the scorpion."

They blink at me and let it sink in. It's their turn to burst out laughing. "We taut..." Marta begins. "We taut, ahhh, Ha! Ha! Ha! We taut the scarpion had roon up your leg! We taut you were takin' it rahther well!"

We laugh together. Ah, the beauty and grace of safari guiding. When the laughter subsides I ask, "Did you guys get any photos?" Andy's father and friend shake their heads.

"Shame, no," the uncle quips.

Marta chuckles. "We were too busy worryin' about it stingin' you under your pahnts to take photos."

I smile at them. "Good. That means I can deny *everything*."

Chapter One: Mortality Moments

<u>*NKOSI:*</u> My Jewish Mother's Worst Nightmare

<u>Nkosi on Platt, different day</u>

Execution Valley

Buffalo calf

Execution Valley

Herd heading to Execution Valley

Chapter Two: TIA

<u>Something Killed</u>

<u>Ahead is a whirlwind of sand…</u>
(photo by James Rowley)

<u>What could possibly be worth this battle</u>
<u>of blood and certain death…</u>
(photo by James Rowley)

They are each other's entire universe…
(photo by James Rowley)

The Call of the African Wild

Mat! Mat! Come quick!...

Chapter Three: Lizard Loves

The Dream Dragon

Dream Dragon Dash

The Dream Dragon

A Reptile Dysfunction

Big O.

Chapter Five: Elephant Memories

<u>Peanuts for Elephants?</u>

<u>Norman in Musth, Different Day</u>

George: Part II

He is no more than twenty yards out…

George turns toward us and opens his huge ears…

I consider him, and him, me…

A sudden sadness grips me. I can't help but think he was trying to bridge the gap between us…

George: Part III

George…occupying a place of honor…

CHAPTER FOUR

SAVING LIVES, AFRICA STYLE

WRECKAGE

*W*reckage. It is the only word that comes to mind as I stare in abject disbelief at the giant, steel carcass of the flipped-over truck. It lay like a dead dinosaur just off the byway. At least a hundred Zambians scramble on top of or alongside it. The bulk of them scuttle around the head of the dinosaur like agitated scavengers. The truck's cargo, hundreds of bags of maize (the base of Sub-Saharan Africa's diet), scatters the roadside like an atomic maize bomb has exploded.

It is obvious the double-trailer truck went off the steep-lipped road. What happened after that, Max, a mechanical engineer on our truck later explains, is that the driver attempted to pull back onto the road. The back trailer flipped, which caused the first one to flip. That, in turn, caused the cab to flip. Like a snake flipping over from tail to head, each coil created greater force, thus crushing the cab completely. Whoever is in the cab must be dead.

We had been following this truck for hours from Livingstone on our way to Lusaka. In convoy with other trucks from the same company, ironically named HAKUNA MATATA ("no problem," or more popularly known as "no worries"), it was traveling like most trucks on the continent at break-neck speed, perhaps for days on end. About an hour and a half earlier, Brett, a tall, powerfully-built

South African passenger on his honeymoon with his Swiss wife, Charlotte, was busy trying to get a photo of this truck to capture the name of the company. He now stands next to me mesmerized by the almost unrecognizable truck.

Traffic has crawled to a standstill as some motorists have stopped to help. Most just stand and gape. Nick stops the truck. He and Mwai jump out immediately. I consider what my First Aid instructor taught us: "Don't be afraid to help. Even if you feel that you might fail, it is better to try. If you don't try at all, the people who would have survived might not make it at all." It is a daunting prospect looking at the wreck lining the road. Whoever is in the truck cannot possibly be alive and, if they are, it's going to require a lot more than what I know to piece them back together.

Then, of course, there is the problem of AIDS. If the truck's passengers have survived, there is no question there will be blood. Lots of blood. I have no mouth-guard for CPR and a limited number of latex gloves. Truckers are notorious for spreading disease across Africa.

A question once presented to me by my Ethics professor in college pops into my head, echoing the words of my First Aid instructor: "You are on your way to something important. It could be a job interview or a first date with the person of your dreams. Rushing to your destination, you see a young girl drowning in a fountain. If you stop to help her, you are going to be late and might even miss your appointment and not get the job, the girl, the money, etc. Would you stop to save the girl?"

"Of course," I said.

"Then why aren't you?" he asked knowingly. "Every day, everywhere there are people who need saving. Just because you don't see them, doesn't mean they aren't there."

These people I can see—or at least see they need help.

It is Jo who ultimately concretizes the decision for me. "Maybe we should see if we can help," she says just behind me, armed with her huge bag of First Aid equipment. In being intimidated by the scene in front of us, I have forgotten that Jo, a thirty-four-year-old from Canada with deep auburn hair, is a nurse practitioner. She has already performed a hundred different medical tasks for my passengers and other people along the way up from Cape Town.

At Jo's shoulder is one of our newest passengers, Kelly. Kelly, thirty-two and a doctor from Canada, has flaming red hair and, perhaps, is the whitest person I have ever seen in my life. (In fact, when we reach Lake Malawi, a Malawian woman sees her in a bathing suit on the beach and then asks me if I thought Kelly had any blood in her body.) Kelly had already spent the last month in northern Zimbabwe helping out in a clinic there as a general surgeon. She worked wonders for people who never would have had the chance for serious medical attention. Compared to what she saw there, this accident would be nothing special. She also understands the very real danger of AIDS.

I consider for a moment that these people are my responsibility, and I cannot put them in danger. I cannot know what might happen in the midst of the accident scene. I also recognize these women are doctors in a place where the closest doctor is a hundred miles away. I think of my professor's words. I take a deep breath and open the door to the truck. We pile down onto the roadside to enter into the pandemonium.

I hustle toward the front of the truck as the doctors go around the back. No one is standing on that side next to the road. I understand why. The passenger side is crushed as flat as a pancake. If anyone was sitting there, that person will be unquestionably unrecognizable. I shudder just looking at it. One second driving down the road, the next, smashed into bloody oblivion. *Not a helpful thought, Mat*, I scold myself. I round the front of the cab and into the throng of sweating black bodies.

Through the crowd I spot Jo and Kelly pulling on gloves from the First Aid bag. It is obvious they are strategizing about how to best help in the midst of the chaos. Holding the First Aid bag is Mya, twenty-six and a fun-loving Aussie "chick" always up for a brew and a laugh. She now looks as serious and businesslike as she would back in England as the manager of a famous hotel that caters to celebrities. With the doctors present, I'm not sure how I can help, or if there is some other way I can help.

I peer through the crowd toward the cab. I am shocked to see Nick, our driver, already at the forefront of those desperately trying to wrench their way into the cab. A man's voice screams from the depths of the cab's twisted metal. I shudder again. A face appears in front of my own. "Do you have an axe?" I step back from him and his earnestness, shaking my head helplessly. "We need something sharp to make rope with!" he exclaims and moves on to the next face.

"I have a knife!" I yell to no one in particular. I run back toward our truck.

As I pass the back of the truck carcass, I see three men on top of the remaining maize bags. Wielding crowbars, they hack at the straps keeping the maize attached to the truck. I understand why they need the knife; it will take them to Kingdom Come to get through the straps with them.

As I get up to the steps of our truck, the remaining six faces peer anxiously down at me. "Are the passengers of the truck alright?" someone asks.

I don't know what to say as I climb into the truck. "The only good news is that there is someone alive in the cab," I mutter to them. I then begin rummaging through my crate for the knife. *God only knows what he is going to look like or if he'll want to live if we do get him out.* I don't add this, of course. "We're gonna be here awhile, guys." They nod at me, understanding. "We're gonna try our best to help," I say, and grab my large knife from my crate. To their credit, they take this statement as an invitation. They clamber out of the truck after me.

I race back to the masses and search for the man who asked for the axe. He is deep within the throng, helping the group to do something with one of the straps. I jump up onto the bags of maize and hold up my knife for one of the hackers to take it. Apparently they are done with the straps. Now I am a foreigner running around with a huge knife in my hand looking decidedly out of place.

I clamber down to the only people who look more out of place than I. Jo and Kelly, their flaming hair pulled back behind their heads, stand with hands gloved and ready. Mwai, our chef, stands next to them holding our bottle of Dettol (antibacterial spray for hand washing after roadside toilet breaks). Just beyond them, a group of men start to unravel a length of strap.

"We may need you to help us when they pull them out, Mat," Jo says.

"Them?" I ask incredulously.

"There's a man in there they're trying to get out from behind the seat. He keeps yelling something about his wife. I'm not so sure she's alive. We can't hear anything from her," she says.

I get that queasy feeling again in my stomach.

Someone bumps me, and I step back as a line of thirty men forms like stressed ants along the strap. Nick appears from the group like a man possessed. "Grab the line! Everybody! Come on! Grab the line! Pull!" I almost don't recognize my friend, Nick, who pushes guys to the line and then grabs it himself. "Pull! Pull! Pull!" He has become the lead rescuer here on this stretch of Zambian highway, two thousand miles from his home in Kenya.

A surge of inspiration and pride flows through me as I watch Nick and the thirty other men heave and strain against the strap. Their muscles stand out like corded iron beneath their skin. Their white teeth are grit in effort and pain as the straps cut into their hands. These men strain with all their might, battling against all odds for strangers they have never met.

Not five seconds pass, and a loud snap resounds in the air. The men go down hard in unison. Nick is the first up from the ground. He pushes his way back through the people to the cab. They have succeeded in ripping the driver's seat from the wreckage. The crowd flows in behind Nick to look inside. There are far too many people standing around just to catch a glimpse of the human carnage within the cab. It makes me angry.

The driver's seat appears above the crowd, and it is passed like a rock star after a crowd-dive. It lands with a thump on the ground. The crowd roars with excitement. There is no way for Jo and Kelly to get in there if the victims need help. I am overcome with my anger at every rubbernecker I've ever seen.

"Everybody move! Let these doctors through!" I yell demonically. I turn to the other passengers on our truck. "Make a semicircle around us and keep everyone away." I hand my knife to Mwai. I push people out of the way so the doctors can get through, and my passengers bravely move forward and create the barrier against the surging onlookers.

As the crowd parts, the driver, a shirtless man covered in tattoos, stumbles out of the crowd just in front of us. His eye is swollen and the skin above his right armpit has been rubbed painfully off. Other than that, he seems remarkably unhurt. Jo and Kelly grab him. "Sir, please sit down. We need to examine you," they implore. He isn't hearing them; instead, he is crying and raging, "My, God! My wife! My wife! My wife! Please get her! My wife is in there! Please! Please! Please…!"

I practically tackle him and manage to get him to sit on the ground. I hold his shoulders tightly. "These ladies are doctors. They are going to help you, sir." Jo and Kelly poke and prod him to check for internal wounds and broken bones. He doesn't respond.

He rocks back and forth on the ground. Jo and Kelly determine quite quickly that, for all medical purposes, he is alright for the moment, pumped up on adrenaline.

As soon as they are done questioning him, I let him up. He jumps up and tries to push himself into the throng to get at the cab. "My wife! I love her! Please get my wife!" It is unbearable. A couple of my passengers leave the scene. I certainly don't blame them.

I catch a glimpse of the interior of the cab as he pushes back to it. It is a mess of tangled metal, glass, plastic, and unclassifiable material. *No one* could be alive in that. This is going to be much harder with this man present, especially with the condition his wife is assuredly going to be in.

Apparently the local rescuers feel the same way. They pull him away from the cab and back to where we are standing. We coax him to sit down. His hands grab his face and he sobs. It is only the sound of a truck revving its engine that brings me out of my concentrating on the man.

On the road, a truck backs up to the cab. Two men are on top of the cab with huge chains. They are apparently going to try and lift the cab up by pulling it toward the road with the other truck. It seems like a good idea to me. That is, until Max, Jo's boyfriend, bursts through the crowd to us. "Mat! If they do what they are doing, and that woman in there is alive, they are going to kill her. The angles of the chains and the placement of pressures they will exert are entirely wrong!"

"Okay," I respond. "Let's go tell them *not* to do that!"

Max and I run over to the driver who is affixing the chain to the underside of his carriage. I pat the man on the shoulder. I point at Max. "Sir, I'm sorry for interrupting you, but this man is a mechanical engineer. Do you understand me?"

The driver looks at me and nods.

"Good." I nod at Max.

"If you attach the chain on your bumper and not on the top of your truck, the angle at which you will be pulling will only cause the cab to drag into the slope of the road. The chains have to be attached to the top of your vehicle and as high up on the axle of that truck as possible. You cannot do it the way you have it! Do you understand?" Max instructs vehemently.

"I understand," the man says. "But, I cannot attach it to the top of the carriage. It cannot hold the weight."

We nod at him. "Please, sir. Just wait then until we get the woman out of the truck, okay?"

He nods at us. "Yes, yes."

Max climbs onto the cab with the other two men. He starts arguing with them about where they are affixing the chains. I can't help but smile in admiration at Max. He is on top of the truck risking life and limb to utilize his knowledge, not caring if he may appear to be out of place.

I race around the cab once again and realize there are still too many people standing around the cab just for the excitement of it. Both Jo and Kelly have been pushed to the periphery of the throng crowding the cab. It is ridiculous. It makes me even angrier. I no longer care if I am a foreign party crasher. This woman may very well die because people are rubbernecking in the intimate area of the accident scene.

I race over to the crowd and push people back. "Let these doctors through! Please! Everyone not helping, please step back!" I roar. My passengers, several rescuers, and I create a circle that blocks the rubberneckers from the cab.

A man wanders through our phalanx carrying an AK-47. Jo and Kelly frown and step back. I can't discern who he might be by his uniform alone, but I'm hoping he is the police. "Are you the police?" I query. "Can you help us keep these people back?" He looks at me uncomprehending and shrugs his shoulders. I take the risk, gun or no gun: "If you are not helping then, sir, you need to step back and let these two doctors do their job."

He chuckles at me, obviously unmoved. Another Zambian helping us to keep people back says something gruffly to the man. AK sneers but steps back to the edge of the crowd. He gazes uncaringly into my eyes and back at the cab. He doesn't want to miss anything. I can't help but think, *Who carries a machinegun into a crowd of people who is not the police?* At least he isn't shooting at us.

With our line holding, I turn to my right to finally catch a view of the interior of the truck sans the driver's seat. Nick, as the prime rescuer, is inside the cab talking softly to the top of a woman's head. Her left arm is pinned up and back behind her as if it is completely dislocated. The only other thing that is visible is her other arm pinned against the side of her face. Her moans are heart-withering.

Jo puts a hand on my arm. "We need you to put some gloves on, Mat. We are going to need your help, and it is most likely going to be very bloody. First, I need you to go back to the truck and find a blanket of some sort."

I grab one of the men near me and point in his face. "Sir, please make sure no one gets in the way of the doctors. Okay?" He takes up my position, so I race back to our truck and grab a sleeping bag that was donated to the truck the morning before by an ex-passenger. Some might argue it was meant to be.

Back at the cab I lay the sleeping bag on the ground fifteen feet from the opening. I move to Mya standing with her arms spread to hold people at bay. One hand still holds the First Aid bag. I take gloves from the bag and grit my teeth. The prospect of the woman coming out of the truck looking like all the gruesome photos I had seen during my First Aid course but had never seen in real life makes me even queasier. I'm not going to be a great help if I throw up all over the patient. I pull the gloves on and steel myself for the woman's removal from the truck's mangled depths.

I have to push several oglers out of the way to get back to my position behind Nick and two other men yanking bits and pieces from around the woman. She is crying and whimpering, but miraculously alive. Behind us, the husband is being held back by several other men.

The anticipation is unbearable. What her body is going to look like is something I have to keep from my mind. We must deal with what may come. With my knife in hand, the man next to Nick saws ferociously at the crumpled dash board that pins the woman's legs.

After hacking for long, anguished moments, he yanks out a section of the dash with a harsh cracking sound. The woman grunts with the pain. Amazingly, it is what is mostly holding her. Nick speaks softly to her, trying to reassure her. The only way to remove her is by lifting the monstrous weight of the cab off the material trapping her and pulling her out simultaneously. If Max was right, we will succeed. If not…

The Zambian next to Nick shouts up to the men on the cab's underside. They yell to the driver of a tow truck that has arrived and to which they have attached the chains. Someone yells "Stand back!" and the crowd clears away. The doctors and I hold our positions nine feet from the cab. Only Nick is in the cab with the woman.

We hold our breath as the truck revs its engine. It inches forward as the driver slowly releases the clutch. The cab shudders but doesn't move. Several voices scream what must be the equivalent of "Harder!" The driver releases the clutch completely, and the truck jerks angrily forward.

With a horrible screeching of metal and material, the cab lifts up from around Nick and the woman like a scene from *Transformers*. Nick falls backward with her as the cab jerks up and away. We all pull the sleeping bag forward. Nick slides out from under her.

Hooking his hands under her arms, he lays her limp body down on the sleeping bag.

"I need you to stabilize her neck as we examine her, Mat," Jo instructs me. I place my hands at the back of the woman's head and survey the poor woman. She is no more than five feet tall and looks like a chubby little girl. She wears a pink tank-top that is torn, dirtied, and blood-stained. It does nothing to cover her tattooed pot-belly dotted with shards of glass and blood.

It is immediately evident that her left leg is *wrecked*. Her thigh is grossly misshapen, indicating a snapped femur. The only thing that has kept the bone from shooting through her skin of her thigh is the jeans' tightness. Her foot dangles uselessly at the end of her pant leg. It is degloved. The skin is pulled completely back, exposing the bone and sinew of her ankle. It is most assuredly broken in at least two places if not shattered. Blood flows from this wound and from a dozen shards of glass stuck in her skin. Her eyes are swollen almost shut. The skin on her upper lip has been ripped off.

The two doctors efficiently run their hands over her body as they ask her questions. Brett and Mya hold onto the husband as he looks anxiously on. Kelly holds open the woman's swollen eye and asks her name. "Precious. My name is Precious," she whimpers.

"How old are you, Precious?" Kelly asks.

"Thirty."

"What day is it?" Kelly tries.

"I don't know," Precious answers. "We've been driving a long time."

Kelly holds her finger in front of Precious' face. "Please follow my finger, Precious," Kelly commands gently. As much as she can through her swollen eyes, Precious follows Kelly's moving finger.

Kelly seems relieved to find nothing neurological to worry about for the moment. She moves down to Jo who is busy cutting the jeans from the bottom to the top of Precious' leg. I am left with

Precious' swollen face in my hands. "No matter how bad it may seem right now, Precious, you are a very, very lucky woman. These ladies are going to help you. They are doctors. Do you understand, Precious?"

"Praise, God. Praise God!" she cries gratefully. "My leg! My leg!" she finishes.

It is hard not to stare at her bloody and dirtied foot and the deep purple–blue of her distended thigh. As Jo reaches Precious' hip with the scissors, a heart-rending pang of compassion overwhelms me. This poor, gruesomely injured woman wears pink, flowered, little-girl underwear under her jeans. I look down into Precious' face to avoid the underwear.

I look up almost immediately as Kelly shrieks past my shoulder, "Stop that! That is, so, so, so, rude. Stop taking photos!" Behind me, beyond all weirdness, a group of young guys in perfectly pressed out-fits of a Marine marching band has appeared from nowhere. Under the brims of their white hats they are laughing as they enthusiastically snap photos of Precious with their cell phones. I see *red*. "What the f–k is wrong with you people? Where is your humanity?" I roar at them.

Brett shoves them roughly back as do some others. They and a few other "photographers" back away. Once their crime has been pointed out to them, the rest of the crowd decides to get on board. Even a local news group with cameras are directed away from the exposed woman on the ground.

"Give these to her, Mat," Max says, as Jo pours Dettol and water on Precious' leg wounds. He hands me eight pills. Two are Tylenol and six are antibiotics. Judging from the amount of crap and blood in the wounds, Precious is going to need a hell of a lot more than just six. Kelly stands over us. "Precious, are you allergic to anything?" Precious doesn't seem to understand.

I lean over her face. "Precious. This is a very important question. Do you understand me?"

"Yes, yes, I understand," she says quietly.

"Can you take pills?" I ask, showing her the pills.

"Yes, I take pills," she says.

"Okay. When you have taken pills in the past, has anything happened to you? Have you felt funny or had to go to the hospital after taking pills?"

"No, no. I take pills. No problem."

"That's good, Precious. We have a lot of pills to take here. They are going to help you feel better, okay? I just want you to swallow them when you are ready to, okay?"

"Yes, yes, but my leg. It hurt so much," she whimpers.

"I know, but you are doing wonderfully. This will be over soon enough."

I feed her the pills one by one as Jo and Kelly work the splint that has been fashioned from pieces of the truck's wheel flaps. Lying down, with people pulling on her horribly damaged leg, Precious is arguably the best pill taker in the universe. She gets all eight pills down within a couple minutes.

Kelly looks at me intently as she and Jo move down to Precious' feet. "We are going to have to pull on her leg to tie it to the splint, Mat. Hold on to her and don't let her move." I clench my teeth and nod at her. I can't imagine anything hurting as much as this will hurt this woman.

Kelly grabs just above the shattered ankle. Jo squats next to her with the splint ready. Kelly nods at me as I hold Precious' head in my hands. "This is going to hurt, Precious," I say. "But it needs to be done, okay?"

I nod at Kelly. She pulls. *Hard*.

"My leg, my leg, my leeeeeeggggg!" Precious screams. Jo and Kelly deftly wrap it to the splint.

It is done. Precious moans softly, without tears. I am amazed how stoic she is. Anyone else would still be screaming a hundred times louder. I definitely would have been if I hadn't already passed out. Jo and Kelly then wrap her left leg to her right leg to stabilize it.

"You did great, Precious. We just have to get you to a hospital now, okay?" I say softly.

"Uh-huh. Where, where, where is my husband?" she whimpers.

I have no idea where he is. Nick later tells us, either due to his shocked state or because he just didn't care, once Precious was out of the cab, all he wanted was his cell phone. After that was found, all he wanted was his passport. After that was located, he wanted his jack that was used to prop up part of the frame above his pinned wife. "He's right here, Precious. He'll be going with you in the ambulance," I lie to her. There is, of course, no ambulance.

There is, however, a pickup truck that was commandeered by a white gentleman. When I first see him I think, *That must be the skinniest member of The Three Musketeers.* He proves to be the regional director of the CDC. He just happened to be passing by on his way to an International AIDS Day Conference in Lusaka. He slips us a neck brace for Precious. "I'm sorry I can't do more," he says, and then disappears, his cameo role fulfilled.

Jo and Kelly weigh the options. "We're going to have to lift her into the back of the truck," Jo says.

I hold under Precious' head. Using the edges of the sleeping bag, we lift her into the back of the pickup. We pull a blanket over her.

"My leg, it hurts. Please take off the thing you put there. It hurts me," Precious begs.

"We can't, Precious. You've done so beautifully," I say, hopefully for consolation. "Just remember this day, Precious. You should not be here talking to me. It is a *miracle* you made it. No matter how much it hurts in the next few hours, just remember how lucky a woman you are."

She nods ever so slightly. "Yes, yes. Praise God. Praaaise God! Where is my husband?" she asks. I look around and see him stuffing things into a bag. Heavy drops of rain start to fall. Jo and Kelly pull a plastic sheet to Precious' chin to keep her from the coming rain. I point at the husband and mouth to Brett, "*Get him*." Brett, almost carrying the man, brings the husband over. He guides him to a spot in the truck next to Precious. "You take care, Precious," I say, and climb from the pickup.

"God bless you," she says weakly.

In our bloody gloves and clothes we watch the pickup carry Precious and her husband away in the falling rain. We look at each other and the hulk of the wrecked truck. We can see at least two lives have been spared this day. Silent, we pick up our paraphernalia and leave the bloodied materials at the scene of the accident.

The majority of the onlookers have dispersed. Mwai comes up to me and hands me my knife. It bears the colors of the dashboard through which it sawed. I pat him on the shoulder. I smile over at Nick who was unquestionably the MVP of this rescue operation. I had never seen him like this. Aside from the movies, I had never really seen *anyone* like this. As I watch my people climb back aboard our own truck, I am once again overwhelmed with emotion.

I try and understand exactly what the emotion is. I realize that, above all, I am proud to be a member of a group of people willing to take a huge risk with their lives to save a couple of strangers in a place where life can be so cheap. More than anything, it reminds me of the question asked of me almost two decades before. This time, I and my fellow citizens stopped for the "girl in the fountain" and, hopefully, made the difference between life and death.

SPEEDO AND THE BEAST

Hunters say that buffalo are arguably the most dangerous of the Big Five: unpredictable, ornery when provoked and, some say, vengeful. They are the only animal of the Big Five you are allowed to shoot beyond ten yards if it is charging. (Elephants can be shot at fifteen yards if they are charging only because of the size and inertia of their bulk.)

This is due to the fact that buffalo do not "mock charge." All other animals may charge simply to intimidate. If a buffalo is charging, it is going to go through with it. Looking like a big cow on steroids, it is understandable how this one-ton animal might appear harmless. Thus, it is the responsibility of a guide to inform those visitors who come to Africa to respect this potentially lethal animal and its mercurial disposition wherever, and whenever, one encounters it.

It is 2:30 a.m. at Simba Campsite overlooking the expanse of Ngorongoro Crater. Except for the dim lights coming from the toilet blocks and the kitchen area sheathed in protective wire, the campsite is pitch-black. I sit up in the tent and listen for the unmistakable sound of the buffalo as their tongues rip grass from the ground.

When I had entered my tent to sleep at 10:00 p.m., there were nearly forty buffalo on the periphery of the campsite, grazing peacefully. I can still detect their faint activity at a safe distance from my tent. That being recognized, I still put into effect the strict regimen I advise all the passengers to do when out in the wilds of Africa and needing a nocturnal toilet visit.

First, one listens. If one hears anything wandering outside the tent, one stays in the tent. Second, having heard nothing, one unzips the tent and shines one's light in the surrounding darkness. If there are eyes shining in the darkness from any animal's *tapetum lucidum* (the reflective layer behind animals' retina to ensure the maximum utilization of light by the rod cells in the eye), then one stays in the tent. Third, if there are no eyes, one stands up in the tent entrance and shines the light 360 degrees to pick up any other eyes. If there are no eyes, one can leave the tent and take care of business.

As I stand just outside my tent, I shine my light in the buffalos' direction. They are a good hundred fifty yards from me at the southeast end of the campsite. I watch and listen to them masticating away. It is a sound that fills me with a sense of peace, comfort, and privilege. I can't help but think, sadly, how few people get to be out in the wilds of Africa, experiencing the harmony of resting safely among these dangerous but magnificent animals. Because of the distance between us and their complete lack of interest in me, I can see that it will be safe to make my journey.

I stride toward the toilets, my feet making little noise in the soft, thick grass. I breathe in the chill night air. It is, perhaps, the purest air in the world, evidenced by the flowing Old Man's Beard lichen my light illuminates in the trees behind the toilet block. This lichen cannot release pollutants from its system and, therefore, only grows in the cleanest air. My torchlight scans the forest and its lichen as I approach it. It isn't impossible for my light to catch the eyes of a curious leopard hiding behind the lichen. One can never be lax in attention, not even for a moment.

After taking care of business, I once again shine my light all around from the restroom's doorway. Only the snoring humps of the passengers' tents greet my beams. I shine my light toward the buffalo again, still a hundred yards away. They have moved right behind another group's tents. I smile as I walk back toward my tent wondering what they would do if they woke up to see a herd of one-ton beasts grazing right in front of their faces.

I reach my tent and unzip it. It is then that I hear one of the tents near the buffalo rustling. Beams of light from two flashlights bounce off the walls inside the tent like a scene from *Alien*. Not three yards from the back of their tent, a bull grazes noisily. I'm hoping they aren't even thinking of getting out.

It is when I hear their zipper opening that I zip my tent back up. I don't want to shout across the hundred-yard expanse as it may cause the animals to stampede and scare the hell out of the sleeping campers—or vice versa. I know, however, I can't allow the two flashlight wielders to get out of their tent. I jog swiftly in their direction, padding as silently on the grass as I can.

I am fifty yards away when the tent's occupants emerge. A man comes out first, sporting only Speedo underwear and hiking boots, laces untied. His presumed wife follows immediately, exclaiming "Que-est ce que c'est?" (What is that?) over and over again. I start to run toward them as a safer-than-yelling "Ssssssst!" escapes my lips to get their attention. Not hearing me, the man clomps around the tent. He shines his light full on the massive creature not three yards from him. If the buffalo charges, he is a dead man.

I hiss as loudly as I can in my terrible French, "Il est tres dangereux! Retournez a la tent!" (It's very dangerous! Get back in the tent!), and I stop at about sixty feet from them. I'm not going any closer. I have no cover from the animal, and buffalo charge at up to thirty miles per hour.

Speedo turns back to me and shines the light full in my eyes. "Non, ce n'est pas dangereux! C'est un buffalo!" (It's not dangerous! It's a buffalo!).

"Non c'est ne pas vrai!" I hiss. "C'est tres, tres dangereux, monsieur! Allez a la tente maintenant!" (That's not right! It's very, very dangerous. Get back in the tent, now!).

Speedo turns back to the buffalo and shines his light again on the munching animal as if considering this fact. I'm sure he has one eyebrow raised as his wife shines her light at my chest to see my face. She can see I am deadly serious. "Madam. Ce buffalo va a tuer ton marie," I state as matter-of-factly as possible. (Ma'am, that buffalo is going to kill your husband.) She nods vigorously at me and then chatters something to her husband too fast for my comprehension. I understand by her tone that she, at least, has gotten the point.

The husband makes a sound as if he has just taken a bite of a bad croissant. In his mono-themed phrasing he says yet again, "Non! C'est un buffalo!"

I watch the animal as it starts to lumber slowly away from Speedo and his marauding light. It certainly doesn't look dangerous.

His wife gestures at him animatedly and hurries to the tent opening. "Alonsi MAINTENANT!" (Let's go NOW!) she yells ferociously at him. He wrinkles his brow and frowns at her. He casts his light one last time as the buffalo continues munching the grass not fifteen feet from him. Speedo shakes his head and walks dejectedly back to his wife. "Cet un buffalo," he says like a petulant child. He clambers into the safety of their tent.

I breathe a sigh of relief and thank the powers that be that, this time, the buffalo's unpredictability went the peaceful way. I know it's not Speedo's fault he was tempting Fate. It's really his guide who is to blame. A guide must tell one's passengers about the dangers of camping in the wilds of Africa. That being said, I would think one would want to wear more than a Speedo and a pair of boots when going out to meet one of Africa's Big Five. Imagine Speedo trying to explain that outfit at Heaven's Gate.

LARIAM DAYS

Lariam/Mefloquine: A drug used to treat malaria and to prevent malaria in travelers who are traveling where malaria is present.
Seek medical attention right away if any of these severe side effects occur when using Lariam: severe allergic reactions (for example, rash; hives; itching; difficulty breathing; tightness in the chest; and swelling of the mouth, face, lips, or tongue); bizarre behavior; loss of balance or coordination; memory problems; mental or mood changes (for example, anxiety, confusion, depression, hallucinations, mood changes, paranoia, and restlessness)...

Bruce is forty-four, six feet tall, 220 pounds, and a builder from the Northern territory in Australia. He is traveling with his petite, adorable, twenty-three-year-old daughter, Eve, from Melbourne (who looks like a 5'2", ninety-eight-pound version of Heather Graham). They have decided to make this overlanding trip together to reacquaint after a two-year separation with no contact. Bruce and Eve's mother divorced when she was thirteen, but Eve knows that her father is a good-hearted man who tries to be a good father despite some deeply ingrained anger issues and a propensity for drink. She would not have taken this trip with him had he not been a decent father to her in their past.

When I first see them interacting, it is painfully obvious how much he loves his daughter. It is just as painfully touching to see her tiny form next to his behemoth size. With her one little hand on his powerful forearm, they talk as if they are two conspirators planning their next heist. Thus, it is with great horror that I, Eve, and the rest of the passengers watch Bruce descend into a Lariam-induced, paranoid-psychotic break-down that nearly leads him, me, and several others to our deaths.

"Good morning, Eve!" I say cheerfully on our first morning together at Meserani Snake Park, our campsite just outside Arusha, Tanzania. "How did you sleep?" She looks exhausted with little red rims under her luminous blue eyes.

"Oh, I barely slept at all last night. My dad came in from the bar at two and was talking all night, but I'm just fine," she states in her soft-spoken way.

I laugh that her father seemingly wanted to chat with her in his inebriated state about the time they had missed and that, perhaps, he didn't want to miss a moment more, regardless of the time. I say as much.

She smiles tiredly. "Yeah, he was saying some really weird stuff, so I just tried to roll over and get some sleep. I think I got about an hour after he came in. He definitely only got an hour some time this morning."

I laugh again. "Tonight you'll sleep like babies at Kudu camp on our way to the Serengeti."

She smiles back at me in her incredibly sweet way. "No big deal," she mumbles.

I don't think anything of it.

I am used to having big drinkers and party animals on the truck and have learned quite well how to deal with them diplomatically. Leading people through Africa, especially in a group setting,

I obviously need to understand how each of the travelers will fit in, who might be a problem passenger, and who can be relied on in emergency situations. On the way into Arusha proper to do some shopping and last-minute e-mailing before our three-day adventure to Ngorongoro Crater and the Serengeti, I size up Bruce on the truck.

My first impressions of Bruce were contradictory and, with hindsight, could be construed as symptomatic of nuttiness to come. The first thing Bruce said to me as I shook his hand in the lobby of the Boulevard Hotel in Nairobi was, "You shake hands like a girl." He, of course, shook hands like, well, a two-hundred-twenty-pound builder from the Outback. I smiled at him and joked, despite the damage being done to my hand.

"I'll do better next time."

He smiled absently at that and nodded in appreciation. It was Eve that saved the rather odd first meeting with her own bubbly, animated introduction.

The following day, the first of what was supposed to be a thirty-six-day trip for him and Eve to Johannesburg, Bruce was very helpful packing the truck. Almost sprite-like in his enthusiasm, he used his obvious strength to help the other passengers place their bags in the appropriate compartments. He asked several times if he could help me, Nick, and Mwai prepare for our departure. I could see he genuinely, good-naturedly wanted to help and be a part of the trip.

I thought our initial encounter the evening before simply may have been a question of different humors from different cultures. Perhaps, as I would later learn, he was simply tired from his stay in Egypt the week before. I reasoned any misbehavior on his part, beer-induced or otherwise, like the introduction, would be mollified by her presence. With twenty-five other passengers to worry about on this trip, it would almost be a necessity.

We come back from Arusha to the campsite, and I am counting the money for the Serengeti on the truck. Bruce comes up and sits across the table. I continue to count and shoot a glance at him. He looks like sh-t. His two patches of hair on either side of his bald spot are standing at all angles. His eyes are bloodshot and half-closed.

"What's up, Bruce? I heard the bar got to you last night!" I say jovially.

"It was the Freemasons, you know," he says vehemently. "We Christians got to stick together. You know that, right?"

I look up from my counting and smile. I wasn't really listening to him. "I'm sorry, Bruce, are you a Freemason?"

He looks at me very seriously, offended. "I am a Christian, Mat. My father was a Freemason. I would never be a Freemason. They are the enemy."

As bizarre as he sounds, I want to be respectful of any religious affiliations he may have. "I see. I'm sorry."

He waves it away with his thick hand. "I need a nap."

"Well stretch out there on the seat, my man. We don't leave for another hour or so. You have plenty of time to nap."

He nods at me and looks at the seats, hesitating. He makes as if to stretch out and then immediately sits rigidly back up. "I don't know…"

I look at him over the money again. He shifts his gaze past my shoulder out the window. After an awkward moment, I turn to see what he is looking at. There is nothing there that I can readily determine.

"Freemasons versus the Christians," he blurts, his eyes far away.

I stare back at him. "Are you alright, Bruce?"

His mind comes back to the truck, and the glassiness disappears from his eyes. He smiles a secretive little grin at me. "Yeah, you wouldn't understand. Don't worry. It'll be fine." With a motion that belies his bulk, he jumps up and shoots down the truck's stairs.

I stare after him and say aloud, "What the f–k was that? I'm gonna have to watch that one."

I have *no* idea how right I will be.

It is twenty-four hours later, deep in the Serengeti, that I realize Bruce's crazy elevator has hit the top floor. The twenty-seven passengers have all been split up into four, eight-seater Toyota Land Cruisers with removable tops for game-viewing. I am in the second vehicle of the day when we pull up four yards from Bruce and Eve's vehicle. (I usually divide my guiding time between the vehicles on this trip, and I was scheduled to be in Bruce's vehicle the following morning.) They are stopped under an umbrella-thorn acacia where all the passengers are either staring at or snapping photos of the most fortunate leopard sighting I have ever experienced. A large, male leopard lays five yards directly above us in the tree, totally unmoved by everyone below gawking at him—everyone, that is, but Bruce.

Bruce stands like a colonel at the front of the vehicle with binoculars plastered to his face. The binoculars are upside-down and backward. He stares out across the Serengeti's expanse at what I can now only assume is a pack of marauding Freemasons or Christians.

"Bruce?" I chortle. "What are you looking at? The leopard is right above us, my man!"

Bruce drops the binoculars from his eyes. He spins his head like something out of *The Exorcist* and fixes a menacing glare at me. "So, you want to change the rules on me, do you? I know what the game is here. I know damn well what the game is. You just go ahead and change the rules. I'm onto it, you bastard!"

I'm more than a little shocked. I look at the other passengers in Bruce's Cruiser to see if they are as shocked as I am. Just as shockingly, they are *not*. Their somber faces convey that Colonel Crazy has been at this all day. Eve's tiny form is in the back window crumpled up, her face in her hands, her shoulders betraying her tears.

"Is everything okay, Bruce?" I ask, a queasy feeling butterfly-ing its way into my stomach. The last thing I need is a drunken, angry, abusive, and large man in the middle of the Serengeti making the trip hell for everyone else. Not to mention the campsite we will be occupying has no fences around it and anything, and I mean anything, can come through it in the middle of the night. (In the past, one group was fortunate enough to experience a pride of lions taking down a straggling buffalo in the middle of the campsite. At dawn, the herd had trampled its way through and around the ter-rified campers in their tents. They had to remain in their tents for most of the morning until the lions finished feeding.)

Again Bruce raises the binoculars, still upside-down and back-ward, to search the horizon for enemies. "I know! I know!" he responds angrily.

Fortunately, the campsite is ten minutes from the leopard sight-ing. (Who would ever think that that would be a good thing?) We reach the camp at sunset. It is a two thousand square yard clearing with a block of tiny buildings housing squat toilets; somewhat pre-posterously, showers; and a large area for cooking within a wired cage. Other than this, acacia-dominated woods and tall grass stretch away from us in every direction. There are several other groups already putting up their tents.

As I disembark from the Cruiser planning to find out what is wrong with Bruce, Mary, a thirty-seven-year-old reconstructive surgeon from New Zealand, preempts me by darting over, her eyes watering her distress. "Eve doesn't want to stay with her father. He has been absolutely awful to her all day, telling her that she is ruin-ing his trip and threatening that he is not going to let her ruin the rest of it."

"Has he been violent to you guys?" I ask, staring over at Bruce who is busy rummaging aggressively through his bag of stuff, as if he is searching for the Holy Grail.

"No, but he's a huge guy, and he is very angry for no apparent reason. It's really scary!" she says.

I put a hand on her shoulder. "It's okay. Eve can stay with you. I'll stay with Bruce and keep an eye on him for the night. Is he at all rational?"

"Sometimes, but he really seems psychotic. My dad thinks it might be psychosis brought on by Lariam. That would be my diagnosis as well if this isn't his usual personality," Mary says.

I'm hoping neither.

"What about you, Mat?" Mary asks concerned. "Do you think it's safe to be in a tent with him?"

It's a darn good question. "It'll be alright, thanks. Someone has to stay with him, and I've taken enough karate and jiu-jitsu to hold my own, even against someone his size," I assure her. She isn't assured at all.

Two minutes later, it is with an even greater sickening feeling that I hear sixty-seven-year-old Rich, Mary's father (also a reconstructive surgeon), say with some urgency, "I think Bruce is suffering a Lariam-induced psychotic breakdown. He is completely paranoid, mostly irrational, and slips in and out of delusional perspectives, believing we're out to get him."

Huge and paranoid. Wonderful combination.

Rich's wife, Ann, a former psychiatric nurse who, incidentally, was present at the first heart transplant in South Africa during her first nursing years, says compassionately, "It's very sad. He has just been terrible to his daughter all day, the poor thing."

I nod at her. "I'm sorry for you guys as well. I'll see what I can do for him."

Rich's next words don't exactly calm my worry: "I think he's beyond help we can provide here, Mat. He needs to be sedated."

Punching Bruce in the jaw or spin-kicking him in the head is about the only sedative available in my arsenal of medications at the moment. I scan the campsite for Bruce and Eve. Bruce continues with his search for the Holy Grail in his bag, and Eve stands with Mary a few yards away from Bruce, casting furtive glances at him. I beeline over to them. "Mary, may I have a word with Eve, please?"

Mary nods and moves away, eyeing Bruce as if he might jump up and race after her. "We'll put you in the tent with Mary, and I'll stay with your father, okay?" I say to Eve.

She nods, her eyes filling with tears. "I don't know what is happening with him. I've never seen him like this!" she cries.

"Rich and Mary believe this is brought on by Lariam, his malaria drug, which is known to have the side effect of psychosis for some people. He is taking Lariam, right?"

She nods enthusiastically, hoping it is the Lariam. "He took his third pill yesterday and two in Egypt each week we were there before coming here," she adds.

I nod, hoping that it's in a reassuring manner. "I promise I'll try to keep him safe, Eve, alright? But I need to ask you some questions." I watch her closely to see if she will lie to me to protect her dad or maybe herself. "Is he violent or has he ever hurt you?" I ask.

She shakes her head emphatically. "No! He has never hurt me. He is very proud of that fact because his father abused him badly. He has had anger management problems in the past. It's part of the reason my parents split up."

A stab of pity for Bruce courses through me. It's understandable now why Freemasons are the enemy. "Has he ever been in jail for assault or been in fights that you know of?"

She nods. "Yes. He has had many fights, although I don't know if he ended up in jail. I haven't seen a lot of him since the divorce, and I haven't seen him at all in two years." The tears begin to fall again.

I put a reassuring hand on her shoulder. "It's okay. It's not his fault. Just keep remembering, it's the Lariam. Let's tell him you want to stay with the girls in case you need to use the restroom in the middle of the night and want one of them to go with you, okay?"

She nods.

"We need to get through to him that we are in an emergency situation due to the Lariam, alright? We need him to understand that we are here to help him."

She nods at this as well and wipes the tears from her eyes. "I'm so sorry about this, Mat," she says.

Sweet kid. I can't help but smile at this. "Don't you worry about it. It's not a problem, Eve," I say reassuringly.

Boy, do I get *that* wrong.

"How are you feeling, Bruce?" I ask as non-confrontationally as possible as we walk over to him. I pick up the tent poles to help him put up the tent.

"It was too long, you know? I came here with my daughter, and I just wanted it to be a nice relaxing vacation, you know? I just wanted us to have a nice time and get to know each other again without all this driving around and the game and that stuff, you know? Just too many people, too much driving, too much game. I just want Eve and me to have a good time together. I don't get to see her hardly often. Just a good time," he says somewhat petulantly.

"Eve's going to sleep with one of the girls tonight so they can go to the bathroom together. I hope you don't mind if I bunk with you."

He looks at me, emotionless. "Yeah, no problem, Mat." He seems calm for the moment, even rational.

"Bruce, do you feel that you aren't yourself today or maybe even the past couple days?" I ask, holding his eyes with my own.

"Yeah. I'm really tired with all this driving around and all these people and the game. You know?"

"Bruce, we all think that you might be suffering from the side effects of Lariam, the medicine you're taking for malaria prevention.

Does that make sense to you?" He pouts like a four-year-old and shrugs his huge shoulders. It would be hilarious if the situation wasn't so dire. "Can I be honest with you, Bruce? You seem like a man who would want honesty." He nods yes. "You scared some people, including Eve, today. We all thought you were acting a little crazy, and I'm scared for you. I believe we are in an emergency situation because of the Lariam. Do you understand?"

His eyes dart from me to Eve. She nods sadly at him. "I didn't hurt you, Eve! I didn't lay a hand on you, did I? I would never lay a hand on you," he insists, becoming animated.

"No, Dad, you didn't. I know you wouldn't! It's just you're acting very angry for no reason, and I'm worried about you."

I interject, not wanting him to come unglued. "Do you know where you are, Bruce?" His eyes shift slowly to me, the anger dissipating.

"Yeah," he says with the same fervor as someone stuck in an insurance seminar. "The Serengeti."

I try not to laugh. "Good. Do you understand that if the Lariam makes you crazy out here, it could be extremely dangerous?"

"I know what's happening, Mat. I'm not stupid. I know what's happening," he answers as if I had asked him what color the sky is.

Eve and I exchange a look of minor satisfaction, but I'm not a hundred percent convinced. "Don't worry, bud, it'll be fine. Dinner will be ready soon. We'll have a delicious dinner and then go to sleep. Tomorrow we'll try and see something really cool, hopefully a cheetah. Would you like to see a cheetah?"

He looks at me almost sane. "I gotta piss. Where's the toilet?" he asks.

So much for the cheetah. "I'll show you," I answer.

Everybody else has an idea that something is wrong. The passengers watch me lead Bruce toward the toilet block, which sits right on the edge of camp. The camp is packed with at least a hundred people and about fifty tents. In fact, it is the most people I've ever seen in this campsite. "I'll wait for you here, Bruce," I say and stop just before the toilets.

"Sure," he says and goes around the small wall that blocks the toilets from the campsite.

I am plotting all the possible outcomes and contingencies for the evening and the next day if Bruce gets worse; then I realize that it has been over five minutes since Bruce had entered the toilet block. I go around the wall and see both doors to the squat toilets are closed. "Bruce?" No answer. I knock on both doors. "Bruce!" I yell. Still, nothing. In a panic, I push the doors open. He's gone. "F—k!" I yell and jump around the wall to peer into the campsite. In the fading light, I can't see him among the tents or people. Better to have looked in the worst place first, I reason.

I run around the toilet block and search the woods. Sure enough, fifty yards out, Bruce is standing with his hands on his hips yelling something into the encroaching darkness. I look in every direction for possible predators, buffalo, or elephants. "Bruce! Don't move!" I yell. He barely turns as I race over to him. It is the fastest fifty yards I've ever done in my life.

"What the hell are you doing out here? We have to go back into the camp immediately."

He raises an eyebrow at me. "What about Ross Blake?" he asks and nods toward the trees.

"What? Who the hell is Ross Blake?"

"*Who's Ross Blake*? I'll tell you who *Ross Blake* is. I saw him this morning at the camp, and he said we'd be sorting things out between us. He's out there, somewhere." He turns back to the trees. "I know you're out there, Ross, you bastard! I know you're out there, and we got business to sort out, my old friend."

I am astounded at the absurdity of it. "Bruce!" I yell. "You can't be out here, my man, remember?" I put a hand on his shoulder. "You don't want to get eaten by a lion, right?"

He looks at me, genuine fear in his face. "No, definitely not." With a tight grip on his shoulder and checking in all directions, I walk him back to the front of the toilets. Fortunately, he doesn't fight me. I'm more than ready to punch him in the chin.

"Bruce, we are very worried about you. Do you understand why?" I ask him.

"Ross Blake," he says. "He owes me money. Took me for fifteen thousand ten years ago when we started our business together. He's over there, and I was just going over to sort him out." He says it so confidently, I almost believe him.

"No. Not Ross Blake. He's not here. We're in the Serengeti, remember? Please listen to me. Eve is very worried about you, and so am I. The doctors and I think you are suffering a breakdown from your malaria drug. Do you understand?" I ask, looking into his eyes. They are far away.

"Yes. I understand."

I grasp his shoulder. "Do you understand that we have an emergency situation here, that you can't go wandering off into the night or you are going to get yourself killed?"

He nods his head tiredly and looks at me. He is back. "Yeah, Mat. Sorry. This is an emergency. We are in the Serengeti."

That will prove to be the last sane statement I hear from him, ever.

Bruce is calm and hasn't said anything, excluding several Cro-Magnon grunts in about an hour. He sits and eats his dinner, several people trying to chat with him. Talking to others, but keeping an eye on him nonetheless, I can see he is still back from the abyss. Checking one last time to see that he is engaged in conversation, I wander off to see about tea and coffee for everyone.

Not three minutes later, I return to inform everyone that it will be ready soon. I scan the dinner area and the people present. There is one missing. "Sh–t." I turn to Jerry, a sixty-seven-year-old American, who had been chatting with Bruce. "Where's Bruce?" I ask.

Jerry shrugs his shoulders. "He went that way," he says and points toward the bathrooms. "Sh–t," I say aloud once again.

"You want me to come with you, Mat?" Jerry asks gallantly.

"No, thank you." I turn on my headtorch and race for the toilets.

Bruce, of course, is not at the toilets. I don't even bother to look back into the campsite. I just know he's on the prowl for Ross Blake. Ol' Ross could only be in one place. I shine my light out into the surrounding darkness of the trees. I want to see if there are any predators' eyes reflecting my light.

I hear a branch crack, and a "F–k!" comes from the darkness to my left. It takes me a second to find Bruce on the other side of an acacia thirty yards out in the bush. I shine my light in every direction to catch the glint of any eyes. Luckily, the usually curious hyenas and lions haven't found their way to the campsite. "Stay there," I say to him.

I sprint over to him and grab him by the shoulders. "So much for the emergency, huh?" I don't wait for his response. I start dragging him back to the camp.

He jerks away from me and stabs his hands to his hips. "What about Blake and the money?" he insists.

A red film creeps across my eyes. "If Blake's out there, he's lion bait and you're never gonna get the money back. Is it worth dying for?" I yell, a couple inches from his face.

With eyes wide open, he considers this. "He's not sane, Mat, remember?" I scream inside my head.

It occurs to me that I might need to try a different approach. I figure if you can't beat 'em, join 'em. "I tell you what," I say. "Tomorrow when we get up, we'll go look for Blake. He can't go wandering off into the night any more than we can, right? If he's around in the morning, you can sort things out. I'll even help you. How does that sound?"

That seems reasonable to him. I lead him back to the toilets, shining my light into the darkness around us. When we reach the toilets I stop him. "You look very tired, and so am I. Shall we go get in the tent and go to sleep?" I query.

"I gotta use the sh–tter" is his response. I watch him very carefully go in and come out of the toilet door. When we reach the tent, I watch him crawl inside. I check my watch. It is 8:30 p.m.

9:40 p.m. Bruce sits straight up from where he was lying on his back, like a man possessed. His movement wakes me up instantly. My hands curl into fists instinctively, ready to deliver some medication if necessary. The camp is still alive with many voices. He, surprisingly calm, says, "It's f–king loud out there. I think I'll go tell them to shut up."

I sit up on my elbows. "No, no, they'll quiet down in a few minutes. I'm sure you're tired enough to sleep through it, right? Aren't you tired? You only slept an hour last night, right?"

He looks over at me like I'm conning him. "No, I am tired. I bet Ross Blake's tired, too," he says. He scooches his butt to the mesh of the door and yells out into the campsite, "I know you're tired, too, you bastard! We're gonna sort this out in the morning!"

10:08 p.m. "Are you a Christian, Mat?"

I open my eyes and look at him curled up in fetal position, looking over at me. "No, I grew up Jewish," I say tiredly, trying to convey to him that he should be sleeping. "Good! You're not a Freemason, then. That makes you as good as a Christian. We Christians need to stick together!"

"Amen," I say.

2:00 a.m. "Mat, I gotta pee," Bruce says, sitting up and looking at me. "Can I go?"

I wake up and look at him through the fog of sleep. I take it as a good sign that he asked me. "Sure, bud. Let's go through the routine and make sure nothing that will kill us is out there." As I tie on my boots, we listen. There is nothing. We unzip the tent and shine our lights into the darkened campsite. Only the sounds of snoring campers indicate there is any life out there. I stand in the entrance of the tent and shine my light into the wilderness behind us. Nothing. "Okay, Bruce. Let's do this."

I help him out of the tent and walk him to the edge of the campsite. He unzips and fumbles about to get himself ready. I make sweeping motions with my headlamp. After about fifteen seconds, he starts peeing. At twenty seconds, I stop at 120 degrees to our right, thirty yards out. Two, deep-red eyes reflect my light back at us. The eyes hang below a tawny shoulder, low to the ground. My blood turns to ice.

"Sh-t!" I hiss. "Let's go! There's a lion!" I grab his elbow.

He jerks it away. "F–k him! I'm peeing!" Bruce yells at the top of his voice. I'm sure the whole camp heard that newsflash. I continue to shine the light in the lion's eyes. Lions like light in their eyes about as much as we do, if not less. The animal holds its position, trying to avoid the light in its eyes by moving its head.

Bruce flicks, flicks, flicks and zips up. "I don't give a sh-t about any lion!" he yells to the animal in my light.

I do. I grab him firmly by the elbow and turn him back to the tent. Someone yells for us to shut the f–k up. "Emergency situation here, remember, Bruce?" I push him toward the tent and follow him backward, the lion's eyes still in the beams of my headtorch.

As we reach the tent, he quickly walks off toward other tents to our right. "I just want to go for a walk, alright? Ross's over here!"

I jump in front of him, the adrenaline starting to kick in. I'm all too ready to deck him. "Bruce, you told me you understood where we were and what we need to do here! Are you a man of your word?" I ask. Beneath the Lariam demon, I know he is and hope there's enough of him left to understand that.

"Yes!" he says, offended.

"Good. Then let's go back to the tent and save both of our lives." He allows me to lead him back to the tent.

2:07 a.m. I check to see that he is lying down before I clamber back in the tent. I crawl inside, zip the mesh door, and then I take off my shoes. With one more look at Bruce, I lay down. As soon as my head hits my pillow, he leaps up and unzips the tent. "I'm ouu-uuuttttaaa here!" he yells and, with the agility of a fox escaping its den, he bolts from the tent.

"I don't believe this!" I yell and quickly tie my boots back on. I try to see where he's going even as I pull them on. As predicted, he's heading toward "Ol' Ross'" part of the camp. As I fall out of the tent, I can't help but mutter aloud, "I don't get paid enough for this!" Somebody in the palatial tent behind ours shushes me.

A scream comes from the tents fifteen yards to the left of our tent. I race over there to find utter chaos. Bruce has unzipped a tent and face-dived into its dark depths. The two women that he lays face down on like the center of a capital letter "H" are beating on him and shrieking like avenging Valkyries. Their justifiable pounding on him actually only succeeds in keeping him inside with them. As Bruce shouts "Sorry! I'm so sorry!", they continue to beat on him. "Wrong tent! Wrong tent, you f–king a–hole!"

I grab him by the back of his pants and yank on him. "I'm sorry, ladies! He's not well. He's not well!" I pull him from the tent, and the lady closest to the entrance manages to clock him one last time in the head. "Get out, you freak!" she shrieks.

"I'm so sorry!" I say to her. "He's not well!"

She zips up the tent and shrieks "F–k you, too!"

I grab Bruce by the shoulders and pull him away. Amazingly, his beating has sobered him considerably. I shine my light all around us to see if the lion has become more interested by Bruce's shenanigans. No lion to be seen, thank God.

Once again I lead him back to the tent. There are stirrings everywhere in the camp. I shove him in it before a lynch mob appears. Once in, I tie my shoelace through the zippers. It would take him a year to untie it. He's not going *anywhere* this night. Neither am I.

2:38 a.m. "Hey, Mat, how much do you think it is to get a woman here?" he asks.

I can't help but laugh. "Do you remember where we are?"

"We're in the Serengeti," he answers.

"That's right. There are no prostitutes here, my friend," I respond.

"Yeah, well, how much to get one out here?" he asks again.

"Bruce, first of all, most—if not all—the hookers in Africa have AIDS. Second of all, it would be about a billion dollars to get one here as you would need a chopper, the government's okay to fly into the Serengeti at night, and to make it the girl's worthwhile. I think we're going to have to go womanless tonight. What do you think?"

He frowns. "I don't have a billion dollars."

2:59 a.m. "I know you're gay, and I don't like it one bit," Bruce whispers angrily in the darkness. I realize at that moment I am not going to get an iota of sleep the rest of this night. "Not one bit," he continues. "You want me here for yourself, and that's why you don't want to get girls to come here."

I want to laugh but might burst into tears if I make any noise. "No, Bruce, I like women," I say as seriously as I can. "I mean, think about it. Don't you think I would have jumped you already if that was the case? We've been in the tent for almost seven hours now. Do you think I would have wasted the whole night?" I ask.

He ponders this. "You're gay," he insists.

"Whatever. I'm tired, my man. Stop bothering me and go to sleep. Eve would be angry if she knew you weren't sleeping."

3:08 a.m. "Eve... Eve!" Bruce yells into the camp through the mesh of the tent.

"Stop yelling!" I hiss. "People are sleeping!"

"I want to speak to Eve right now! Eve!"

I can hear the lynch mob scuffling about in the tents of the campsite. "Shut the

f–k up!" rings out from more than a couple tents.

"Shhh!" I admonish. "Do you want to wake her, dude? You kept her up the last two nights, and now she needs her sleep, right? You want her to sleep and be happy, right?" I pull out the doubting-the-love-for-his-daughter card.

Yeah, I want her to sleep," he says softly.

"You're a good man, Bruce," I say good-naturedly.

"That's right," he says. "I *am* a good man...and *you're gay!*"

3:24 a.m. *Boop! Boop! Boop! Boop!* Bruce has his cell phone out and dials away. I can't even imagine who he is calling. In my tired stupor, I don't even care. In fact, a part of me can't wait to hear his conversation.

"Nora!" he shouts into the phone. "Are you here in the camp, honey? You're *where*? The Philippines? I thought I saw you in the camp here...No, I'm not mad at you. I love you! I'll see you at Christmas time... I do love you, Nora. Why don't you come into the tent? What? You're not here?" He looks out the tent window. "But I see you over there. You look so beautiful in the moonlight...What? No! Just take a left at the moon, then walk twelve degrees over to the tree and we're right there. It's easy, honey! Just come right in. Mat was just leaving."

"Bruce," I implore, not wanting to understand the bizarre and probably sad relationship he must have with this Filipino. "If you want to see Nora at Christmas, you better get off the phone. This call is going to cost you your plane ticket there, you know?"

He looks at me for almost five seconds, weighing his options. This might be another one of my *gay* tricks. Finally, he nods. "Nora, honey, I love you. I have to go. If you want to come into the tent, just come in. Mat can leave when you come in."

I'd have been happy to.

3:38 a.m. *Click-click! Click-click! Click-click!* The beam of light flicks on and off the ceiling of the tent.

"What are you doin', Bruce?" I ask as nicely as I can.

"I need a woman," he says. "I need a root right now!" He sits up and looks out the mesh at the light in the caged kitchen. It is one of the cooks starting to prepare our 5:00 a.m. breakfast.

"Bruce, that's one of the cooks making breakfast. What do you say we get an hour of sleep?" I request, beyond ready to kill him.

He sits up and starts making a square on his torso and crotch with the flashlight. "I'm right here, ladies. Come and get me!" he screams.

Who could resist such an offer?

Apparently, every woman in the campsite. Amazingly, I'm laughing again. "Does that ever work for you?" I inquire.

He points the flashlight at me. "You just better get out when she comes over."

"I'll do that," I respond. "But only when she comes over."

I wake up at 5:00 a.m. I get about an hour and five minutes of sleep. The last thing I remember before falling into an exhausted coma is Bruce sitting up with a fist on his hip and the other shining the light on his crotch. "Come and get it, ladies. Come and get it! I want a root!"

When Eve comes over at a quarter past five, Bruce awakens and begins dry heaving in the tent. I unzip the tent and he flops himself out the door. "I need some fresh water. Mat poisoned my water!"

Eve looks at me with consternation. I smile and shake my head. I offer her my bottle and nod toward him. "Watch. I'll drink some, Eve will drink some, and then you can drink some, okay?"

He watches us intently. We don't die. I hand him the bottle. He looks into it and takes a drink. "Eve will take you to breakfast while I put down the tent, okay, my man?" He's off to breakfast as fast as I've ever seen a two-hundred-twenty-pound person move.

I watch him carefully at breakfast to see if we are going to need to take him directly back to Arusha. We would have to split everyone else into the remaining vehicles, or worse, helicopter him out, which is possible but awesomely expensive. He eats his breakfast, and possibly several other people's breakfast with great gusto. He then ensconces himself in the backseat of the Cruiser. Mercifully, he immediately falls deeply asleep. No helicopter necessary.

Three hours later we find a cheetah beneath a tree, two hundred yards from the truck. Camouflaged in the brown grasses in the shade of the tree, it is difficult to see well, even with binoculars. Bruce appears in the roof with us, wide awake. He again applies the binoculars upside-down and backward. "I don't see sh-t!" he declares.

I turn his binoculars so he can see properly. "Right there, under the tree." He focuses the binos, but he is looking in the wrong place. I try and move the binos so he can see. "Do you see it now?"

"No!" he says vehemently. "Let's go over there."

I don't want to get him riled, but it isn't possible to off-road in the Serengeti like most national reserves or game parks. Off-roading destroys the terrain and its denizens. I explain as much to Bruce. "I'll tell you what," he declares. "John Wayne would go over there."

A laugh escapes me. "What?" I ask incredulously.

"Yup. John Wayne woulda gone right over to that cheetah. Not that I have any respect for that pink-panty-wearing motherf–ker!"

Everybody in the vehicle exchanges glances, flabbergasted. "We can go," I say to the driver before Bruce has any other great, John Wayne-inspired ideas.

Five hours into the morning, we stop at Naabi Hill Gate (where one checks in when coming into the Serengeti from the East) for lunch before heading back to Arusha. Eve and I climb to the top of Naabi Hill overlooking the vast expanse of the Serengeti. Eve calls her father's insurance company in Australia and hands me the phone.

The nurse tells us that it may take eight days for the Lariam psychosis to wear off and that we must take him to the hospital as soon as possible.

"Is there a hospital where you are?" the nurse asks.

I laugh. "Ma'am, if you could see what I'm looking at right now you would laugh. I'm standing on a hill overlooking the Serengeti in Tanzania.

"How nice!" she blurts.

"Well, it's nice except for the fact we're at least six hours from a hospital that can handle him," I state. *I'm not even sure there is a hospital that can handle him.*

"Well," she says, "You better get him there as soon as possible."

Sounds good to me.

On the way back to Arusha, Bruce slips in and out of consciousness. Any time he is awake, Eve and I try to engage him in conversation about anything. We stay away from topics like Freemasons and John Wayne. About a third into the trip, he sits straight up and leans back down.

I put a light hand on his shoulder in case he makes a break for it past Ann, Rich, Jerry, and Mary seated in front of us, and out a side door. After three up-down exercises, he rests in the seat with his arms crossed over his chest. A minute passes with him sitting calmly, staring straight ahead, and seemingly lost deep in thought. I remove my hand from his shoulder.

As soon as my hand comes off, he jumps up with a triumphant "Ha, ha!" and unhinges the two rubber levers that hold the portion of the roof above us onto the vehicle. The roof flies open, squeaking loudly under the force of the eighty-kilometer-per-hour wind. Fortunately for the truck directly behind us, that portion of the roof has metal hinges at the back. It would have flown off our vehicle like a giant ninja star and decapitated everyone in that vehicle. Bruce giggles like a child as we reprimand him.

Everyone had been doing a wonderful job tolerating him, perhaps realizing that he isn't himself. After reaffixing the roof, Ann turns around and smiles gently at Bruce. "Bruce. You know you can't do that, honey. That is dangerous for all of us."

Bruce blinks at her and, before I can pull him back, he shoots forward and wraps his huge arms around her seat and her. I pull back my fist to punch him in the side of the head when Ann exclaims, "Oh, Bruce. You're such a sweetie!" She pats him on his forearm, and he hugs her.

"I'm sorry, Mum. I won't do it again. We're going to be alright, aren't we, Mum?" he asks.

"Yes, we are, Bruce. Now just lay back there and enjoy the ride back to Arusha. Try and take a nap." Bruce miraculously lays back, smiling lovingly at Ann.

It takes three or four hugs and several professions of his love for Ann for us to realize that Bruce believes Ann is his dead mother. I question Ann with my eyes to see if she is comfortable with this lunacy. She nods at me calmly indicating that it is fine. It proves to be anything but.

Upon reaching Meserani, I advise Eve and Bruce to shower before the taxi arrives to take us to the hospital. Bruce says he doesn't need one (he definitely does after three days without one), but Eve gets her cosmetics together and heads off to the showers. I leave a seemingly calm, if not a little confused Bruce with the other passengers to see about the taxi.

At the office at Meserani, I inform Ma, the owner of the campsite and perhaps the sweetest, most helpful person in Africa (if not the world), about the situation. I request that she directs us to the best hospital in Arusha and to procure a taxi. In her usual kindly fashion, she arranges everything. I thank her and step from the office into chaos.

Just outside, Bruce has a death grip on a hysterical Eve's arm. He is dragging her away from passengers who are trying to get him to let go of her. I race over to them with my arms raised above me, the same motion I would use to dissuade a charging elephant. "Bruce!" I yell. "What's up, my man? What's *up?*"

He shoots his blazing eyes to me and back to the other passengers, and then he yanks on Eve. She screams through her tears, "Let go of me! You're hurting me, Dad!" I realize immediately that if he is willing to hurt her after a lifetime of not, the camel's back is broken and it is medicine time.

"We have a security breach here, Mat!" Bruce screams and points at the other passengers. "They're trying to kill us! The war has started!" Eve wrenches her arm from his and bolts around the bar-office. He moves to follow but I jump in front of him, waving my arms. "Come on, Bruce! You know we are in an emergency situation here, remember? No one is trying to kill you. That's the Lariam speaking!" I say loudly, but calmly.

He glares at the other passengers. "All of them! Security breaches!" he roars.

I turn my head to the passengers and yell, "Get out of here, guys. I'll take care of him." They back away but don't leave. I keep myself between him and them. "Tell me what a security breach is. Maybe I can help you determine if they really have broken security," I cajole.

Bruce reaches down and grabs a stick off the ground. He eyes the passengers and then puts the tip of the stick in the dirt. He begins drawing what looks like a bird. "They couldn't draw this. I asked them to draw this and they couldn't do it! They could do it eighty percent but not a hundred." He finishes with a brandish of the stick. It is actually a pretty good picture of a dove. I say as much.

"You think so, huh?" He turns a suspicious eye on me. "Let's see you draw it, Mat."

Oops. He hands me the stick. I put the stick on the ground knowing this may be a defining moment. Picasso I am not. I look at the other passengers; they can't wait to see this. "Go back to the campsite," I say gruffly to them. But they don't.

I draw the dove as best as I can, but it comes out looking like a deformed pterodactyl. Bruce eyes me once again, triumphant in determining that I, too, am a security breach.

"I knew it," he says, clenching his teeth. "Security breach."

I look back at the pterodactyl to try and see how I could have improved it. Bruce steps around me and, with his hands curled into ham-sized fists, heads toward the passengers. "Now, where is my daughter? I know you bastards have her."

"Run!" I roar at them.

Bruce strides determinedly after them knowing that the campsite isn't big enough for them to get away. I trail him, trying to think of something to distract him. I see a scab on the back of his leg and remember, two days before, his asking if it was a spider bite.

"Heh, Bruce! Remember when you asked me about dangerous spider bites here in Africa? I think the one you asked me about is infected."

He stops and looks at the back of his leg. It is enough for me to get in front of him. "I don't care. I need to find Eve and get to the airport!"

He stomps toward the tents, which the passengers are obviously planning on using as a buffer between him and them.

"Someone go find Eve!" I yell. I'm running out of ideas except for the H-bomb to the chin option. Again I wave my arms to distract him. He twists and turns around the tents to find someone from which to extract the information that will lead him to Eve. Everybody moves away accordingly. It is starting to look like a synchronized Vegas show.

"Eve is fine, Bruce." Would I lie to you? You can trust me, right? Who saved your life last night? You remember? Who?"

He stops and looks into my eyes. "I can't trust you anymore, Mat. You've proven to be a security breach." He looks over my shoulder at someone.

"Come on, my man, I saved your life not once, but twice last night. Why would I do that if I was going to harm you today?" He moves as if to go around me, but I step to block him and hit a tent. I stumble, and he beelines for Ann.

As he puts an arm around her, I raise my arms into fighting position and stalk toward them. Ann holds up one hand at me and slides the other around Bruce's waist. "They've got, Eve, Mum, and we gotta get her back!"

Ann nods up at him and pats his forearm again. "Oh, go on, Bruce. Tell me aaaall about it!" The woman is an angel and a brave one at that.

Ann holds onto Bruce's waist as he explains all the security breaches that have taken place as well as the plot to kill them by the Freemasons among us. She nods up to his angry face as if his concerns were her concerns. I turn to see if anyone has found Eve. Blessedly, a couple of female passengers lead her swiftly across the campsite.

"See, Bruce. I told you she'd be here in a few minutes," I say, hoping to gain his trust back.

"Eve!" he cries and races over to her. He attempts to hug her, but she eludes him.

"Don't touch me!" she cries, still visibly shaken.

Bruce is hurt by her command. "Have I ever laid a hand on you? Have I ever laid a hand on you in anger? Have I ever hit you? No! No! I would never hurt you, Eve!" he cries back. It is getting sadder by the second.

"You just did!" she hurls back.

"Don't you understand, Honey?" he screams, gesticulating wildly. "I'm trying to save you! The war is on! They're all trying to kill us. I'm trying to save us. I'm trying to save *you!*" Eve just shakes her head at his insanity and continues to back away from him.

I jump in. "Look, Bruce!" I point to the taxi pulling up into the campsite. "The cab's here to take you to the hosp…, um, airport!"

Bruce turns his attention to the cab. I pick up their backpacks and head to the car, hoping Bruce will follow me. Thankfully he does. He grabs his Holy Grail bag and looks to grab Eve's hand. She skirts him and jogs to the cab. Ann comes up behind us to play her role of supportive mother and to say good-bye.

I nod for Eve to climb into the front passenger seat as I begin stuffing their packs into the trunk. Bruce tries to stop her. "We can't use this vehicle until we check it for nuclear bombs."

"So check it while we put your bags in the car," I say as nonchalantly as possible. He does, beginning with the back seats.

The driver, Godfrey, a bright, smiley Tanzanian comes around to help me put the packs in the trunk. "How are you? I'm Mat." I smile at him.

He shakes my hand. "I'm, Godfrey. Habari [How's it going]?"

"Godfrey," I say, "This is going to be the weirdest taxi ride of your life."

He smiles broadly. "Hakuna matata," he quips. We have no idea how right I am, that what should be a half-hour ride to the hospital will be a five-hour ordeal.

Bruce finishes his check of the vehicle and climbs into the back seat with his Holy Grail bag. I try to climb in after him, but he blocks me with his hip. "Not you, Mat! You've had five security breaches, and I just can't trust you anymore!"

I push against him and manage to get my butt in the seat. I turn my head to him so that our noses are inches apart. "Whether you trust me or not, Bruce, I'm making sure you and Eve get to the airport, safely. It is my job and duty to do so," I say like an actor from *Pearl Harbor*. He raises an eyebrow at this but looks away to slight me.

Ann has her face in the doorway on the other side. "Bruce, it's fine. Your plane is waiting. You be good and let this nice man take you to the airport," she says calmly.

"You wouldn't lie to me, would you, Mum?" he asks desperately.

"No. Definitely not," she says.

"Then you come with us," he implores her.

I shake my head at her behind his back. *No f–king way.*

She smiles angelically at me and then into Bruce's desperate face. "Why not?" she says. "We'll say good-bye at the airport!"

I could tell her a couple thousand reasons "Why not" right off the top of my head.

Much to my horror, she jumps jovially in next to Bruce. Bruce slides into the middle to accommodate Ann. The backseat doesn't have room to flatulate in with Bruce's bulk stuffed between Ann and me. "Let's go, Godfrey!" I cheer. Eve waves to the other passengers who are lined up outside like a funeral procession. Bruce clutches his bag in his lap and stares straight out the window. "F–king Freemasons," he says.

We try very hard to distract Bruce with conversation as we cruise along the byway toward Arusha. He, however, is immersed in finding something in his bag. Ann and I socialize with each other as if he isn't there, both of us watching him like hawks.

Bruce pulls out a soap dish with soap. He opens it and scrutinizes it. "Security breach," he says and chucks it out my open window.

"Bruce!" we yell in unison. "You can't throw things out the window!"

"Security breach. Had to go!" he says like a man protecting the president. He then breaks into a childish giggle. Even when you're insane, it's fun to throw things out of a moving vehicle.

Bruce searches some more in his bag as I roll up my window. He whips out a deodorant bottle. He lifts the cap off. He smells it. *Fwiiinnggg!* He chucks it out Ann's window. "Another security breach. Definitely nuclear!" He laughs like a little kid. Ann rolls up her window.

He then pulls out a shirt, which he dutifully feels for nuclear weapons. "Safe," he says. He turns his head to me angrily. "What are you looking at, Freemason?" I casually look away. He delves into his bag of potential projectiles again, rummaging there for a good two minutes.

I don't even know what he has in his hand when he yells, "Security breach!", leans forward, and flings it past Eve's face out her window.

"Bruce!" I yell, pulling him back. I leave my hand on his shoulder.

"No more of that now, Bruce," Ann scolds, also putting a hand on his shoulder. Her other hand finds his right hand. "Won't you hold your Mum's hand now?" she asks sweetly. He takes her hand and looks at it for a full twenty seconds.

Bruce jerks her hand up in front of her in a bizarre version of a Nazi salute. "We can contact the aliens this way. Yes! Yes! The aliens! Just like that, Mum! Just like that! They'll help us with this war!" he yells in his moment of eureka. "Just hold it like that, Mum, till we get to the airport!"

As worried as I am about Ann's shoulder trying to hold up her new alien-contacting "device," I'm pleased that Bruce focuses on her rather than her window, which displays the airport whizzing by.

Ann rests her hand on the headrest in front of her. "I'm just going to keep it there, okay, Bruce?" Ann asks. Bruce doesn't hear her. He is staring intensely out the windshield at the truck in front of us. He shoots forward and roars, "They're trying to kill us, those trucks! Driver! Get around them, now!"

Godfrey races around the truck more from shock than from necessity.

Apparently, it's not quite fast enough for Bruce. He tries to grab the wheel. Ann and I grab his shoulders and pull him back with every ounce of strength we have.

"Pull over, driver!" Ann yells. This is the first time I have seen her even a little ruffled.

Godfrey actually speeds up, the poor guy, probably thinking the faster he goes the quicker this nut will be out of his cab. I doubt he'll ever drive for Ma again in the future. Bruce starts to fume. "They all have knives along the road! The war is on! They're gonna kill us all! Not my Eve!" He jerks forward from our grasp and tries to grab the wheel yet again. The car squeals all over the byway.

"Pull over right nooowwww!" Ann screams.

Godfrey yanks the wheel, and we veer off the road. He jams on the brakes, and we skid to a halt where a gravel road meets the byway. We hold Bruce as much as we can as he shrieks, "I'm driving now! Give me the keys!"

Not going to happen. We all jump out, and Godfrey bolts about forty yards from the car. He stops to see if he needs to run any farther. Ann moves around the cab to comfort Eve, who has burst into tears. Bruce stands at the car bellowing at Godfrey. I try to distract Bruce with the arm-waving routine again. Above us, a huge flashing billboard invites all leaving Arusha to come visit the Serengeti. Without Larium, I presume.

"Mat!" Ann yells behind me. "He's gone, Mat! Don't bother trying to talk to him. Just let him wear himself out."

I turn to Ann. "I think I'm gonna have to hit him in the chin."

"Just let him be," she advises. "Psychotics are unimaginably strong, and he's already a big man. He'll hurt you. Give him a few minutes."

Bruce turns his rancor at the fifty or so Tanzanians hanging at the crossroads' various stores, fences, and shebeens there. "I know what you all are waiting for," he roars at them. "You're not gonna take us out!" He backs toward the byway, looking all around him as if he were a gladiator in a pit of lions.

"We can't let him hurt anybody or himself," I say to Ann.

I race over to Godfrey. "Call Ma. Have her call the hospital and send an ambulance with sedatives. Do you know the name of this place?"

Godfrey nods nervously. "My phone is in the car," he says.

"Okay. I'll distract him. Have her send them here. *Please* tell her it's an emergency."

He heads to the taxi as I head toward Bruce. He is busy taunting slowing cars in the middle of the byway. "Get out of the road, Bruce!" I shout.

Bruce points up at the flashing billboard. "Ha! You see? The aliens are here to save us. They'll take us way above the nuclear war!" He points to the Tanzanians who are approaching from all angles to catch a closer glimpse of the white madman in the middle of their road. "You're all gonna die, but we won't! Ha! Ha! The aliens are taking us away!"

A short, balding Tanzanian intercepts me as I near the edge of the byway. "He's crazy," the man pronounces astutely.

I'm about out of patience. "Thanks for the newsflash," I blurt. "Please, sir. Step away from here. He is not well," I advise.

He then freezes my blood with his next statement: "I call the police, now." A vision of the police showing up and turning a crazed Bruce into Swiss cheese pops into mind. Calling the police in Africa is not necessarily the best of ideas; most of the time, it makes matters worse. Much worse.

"*Please*. Do *not* call the police, sir," I beg. "This man is very sick, and we're taking him to the hospital."

"You get him off our road, then," he demands.

"Yes. Right now," I promise. I look up, but Bruce is no longer in the road. He's heading straight for Godfrey who sits in the driver's seat speaking to Ma on the phone. "I want those keys! I'm driving," he snarls.

I am twenty steps away when Bruce grabs Godfrey's hands with the keys in them. Much to his credit, Godfrey refuses to relinquish them. The time has come: *medication time*. I am five steps away as Bruce gives up on the keys and goes for Godfrey's neck. I leap through the air, intent on utilizing a standard jiu-jitsu chokehold to take Bruce out. I land on his back and slip my arm around his thick neck. I may as well have been a tsetse fly.

Bruce instantly turns into me and, with what feels like Herculean strength, shoves his shoulder into my ribs. His momentum carries me in the air, backward. He slams me down on my left side into the gravel and follows it up with slamming himself onto me. Before I can realize that I'm not broken in half, Bruce starts hammering my head with his ham-fists. I turn my back to him.

Left ear! Right ear! Cerebral cortex! Bruce connects with the back of my head and ears like a man with a couple of anvils. The only thought that races through my mind, weirdly enough, is *I can't wait to tell my friends about* this *one!*

In the background I hear Eve screeching, "Help him! Please somebody help him! Pleeeeease!" I could definitely use the help.

After beating his fists with the back of my head a half dozen times, I flip around toward him in an attempt to get him in a standard jiu-jitsu control position. As I flip around, however, I realize he sits astride my stomach and above my hips. It is about the worst position to be in.

Fortunately, my adrenaline has kicked in, and I have control of his right arm with my two arms. I have his right elbow pinned to my ringing right ear. I manage to slide my left leg out from under him as he attempts to hit me with his left arm. He only succeeds in scraping all the skin off his knuckles on the gravel. I succeed in swinging my left leg up and over his right shoulder and scraping my boot across his face. Hardly the perfect arm-bar, I reason, but at least I'm no longer having my head used as a punching bag. Suddenly, Bruce is yanked from me as if by an invisible crane.

I leap to my feet and assume a fighting stance. Bruce stands with his arms out wide, several feet away. Blood covers his shirt and drips from his hands and knees. Before I can decide how much of it is mine, he says judicially, "You jumped *me*, Mat! You jumped me! I had to defend myself!"

Thankfully, I can see he doesn't want to play anymore. Behind me, Eve is in hysterics, sobbing uncontrollably into her hands. Poor kid.

I flip around to her and hug her. "It's okay, Eve! It's okay. I'm okay," I comfort, totally unsure of the veracity of that statement. My ears feel like two balloons attached to the side of my head and, for some reason, the world is ringing.

"I'm sorry! I'm sorry! I'm so sorry," she sobs. I pull her away from Bruce who is already on his way to offer supplication to the aliens via the billboard.

"The spaceship is landing!" he exclaims excitedly.

My bald Tanzanian friend appears at my side, waving his phone. "Now, I call the police!" he shouts at me.

I hand Eve off to Ann. "Please, sir, if you call the police, they will come and kill my friend. Please do not call the police," I implore once again.

"Stop fighting then!" He shakes his finger in my face. It occurs to me to punch *him* in the chin. Instead, I offer, "Thank you, sir. No more fighting, I promise. You are very kind."

He strides away to stand with an ever-burgeoning crowd of mumbling onlookers. This story will undoubtedly go down in the history of this junction.

The "ambulance" arrives a half hour later, as a much-subdued Bruce, Ann, and Eve sit Indian-style in a little circle under the billboard, their arms out in front of them, touching. As a security breach, I am not allowed to participate. Apparently, Ann tells me later, this ritual will not only call down the mothership, but it will also help them net billions by rearranging the planets.

Godfrey approaches me and points at the ambulance. "They are here to take you to the hospital." There must be a mistake. Or a scam.

The ambulance is a beat-up Toyota Land Cruiser crudely painted red and blue. Two smashed sirens sit atop the roof. The side of the vehicle reads SECURE SECURITY. Six tall, brawny Tanzanians in dark-blue, one-piece jumpsuits clamber out of the vehicle and affix their military-style hats on their shaved heads. They have batons hanging from their belts. *Secure Security, my ass.* Godfrey gives the seeming leader—a muscular, giant of a man—a wave. They walk over to us. All I can think is, *I don't get paid enough for this sh-t.*

"We're here to help you," the giant says in a foghorn voice.

"Sure," I respond. "Do you know who sent you?" I ask, wanting to make sure that he came from Ma's. We had already been there for over an hour. It wouldn't be impossible for someone to have called these guys to come and take us anywhere they'd like and help themselves to our money, bags, and our lives under the guise of "helping us."

"I don't know. We got call. Here we are."

Of course. "One second, Rafiki," I say to him and his team of giants. I pull Godfrey out of earshot.

"Let me use your phone, please." Godfrey looks at me, questioning. "I'll give you money for the call. I just want to make sure these guys were sent by Ma and the hospital. We called quite a while ago, and we need an ambulance, not a military rugby team." He relinquishes his phone.

I check his list of recently called numbers and see Ma's number. I dial and she picks up. "How's it going?" she asks in her sweet, always concerned way.

"Um, hard to say, really. Tell me. Did you call the hospital and ask for an ambulance?" I ask.

"The hospital doesn't have an ambulance. I had to call a security service. Are they there yet?" she asks.

I look over at the six men staring impatiently at me. I sigh, "They are. Ma, thank you so much. As always, you are an angel. Do me a favor, please? Please tell Mary and Richard from New Zealand that Ann is alright."

"Sure, Mat. Let me know if you need anything else," she says. I hand Godfrey back his phone. *How in hell is this going to work?*

I walk over to the giants of the SS team, a plan hatching in my ringing head. "Thanks, guys, for your patience. Listen. The man we need to transport is very sick. He is very crazy and does not have control over himself. Do you understand?" They nod in unison. There is nothing in the way they do it that conveys they understand. "I am going to tell him that you guys are a security force here to take him and his daughter safely to the airport. We are not going to the airport. We are going to the hospital. If he asks you guys, can you just tell him that is why you are here and nothing else?" I ask seriously.

"Hakuna matata," Lead Giant affirms calmly.

I continue, "If that doesn't work, we will have to subdue him. Do you understand?" They shake their heads, not understanding. I make a fist and pretend to punch myself in the chin. For effect, I roll my eyes back in my head. They laugh and shake their heads excitedly. They like that idea. I really hope it doesn't come to that. These guys could easily pull Bruce apart like jerk-chicken. "I'll be right back," I tell them.

I jog over to about fifteen yards behind Bruce. He is busy making the ladies repeat an alien "OM" and raising their hands to the heavens. The ladies watch my approach. I wave for Eve to come with me. "Dad, I'll be right back to help you, okay? I have to use the toilet, okay?" Bruce responds with a grunt. The mothership must be close. I walk over to the other side of the taxi, and Eve follows me.

"We only have this one chance, Eve, to get your father to the hospital without any further violence. If the plan doesn't work, these men," I point to the SS team, her eyes widening at their apparent bulk, "will have to subdue him."

She animates immediately. "Subdue him, punch him out, do whatever you need to. That isn't my father over there!"

I suppress my laugh. We all have had it. I explain the game plan to her, and she nods, understanding fully that the plan requires her to convince her father that the security force is there to escort them to safety. If it doesn't work, she needs to step back and let them do their thing.

I walk her over to the security guys and introduce her to them. They all smile at her tiny figure. "You ready, kid?" I ask. She's all enthusiasm. "Go get 'em," I offer.

I clench and unclench my teeth as I watch the diminutive general lead her six-man force over to her father and Ann. She approaches her father and gestures toward the security team. Bruce jumps up to greet them, and Ann wisely moves away. I can't hear what she is saying, but as she puts on the hard sell, Bruce looks from her to the security guys and back again. I cross my fingers.

Ten seconds later, Bruce straightens his back, puffs out his chest, tucks in his shirt, and allows the security force to surround him. He is beaming. Like a man on a presidential mission, Bruce allows the retinue to march him over and into the vehicle. I stand there with my jaw dropped open. *It f—king worked!*

Secure Security rolls by us as we clamber into the taxi. Bruce doesn't even cast us a side glance. The Toyota slides onto the byway and hits its lights and siren. I can't help but think that it is at Bruce's request. Ann smiles over at me, "Well! That just worked like a charm!" I'm still too flabbergasted to answer. Godfrey pulls the taxi onto the road leading to Arusha.

When we get to the hospital, Bruce has calmed down almost to the point of being the man I met the first day. I get out of the taxi and walk up to him, still surrounded by the six behemoths. His face is serene and tired. He puts an arm around my shoulders. "I'm sorry if I hurt you, Mat," he says.

I put an arm around his waist and lead him into the emergency reception. "No sweat, my man. I'm glad you didn't hurt me, too. I hope you didn't get hurt." I look at his bleeding knuckles and bleeding knees.

"Ah, it's nothing. I've had much worse." Judging from the chunks of gravel and asphalt in the wounds, I'm not so sure.

At check-in, they give me a card to fill out for him. It asks for the hospital registration number, his name, date of birth, village, tribe, sex and, strangely, years. I begin filling it out and can sense his silence next to me. I look at him. "I want to fill one out," he says like a pouting four-year-old.

I laugh and give him another one. "Do me a favor, my man? Go sit down over there and fill it out." He nods and races over to where Ann and Eve are sitting in the waiting room.

After I finish the paperwork and sort out the bill, Bruce returns brandishing his card proudly. He hands it to me like it is a work of art. It almost is. He got his name right. For the "hospital registration number" he misspells whatever he was trying to convey with "*Cyrstal Disks.*" For "village," he writes "*Mumbo Jumbo.*" For "tribe" he puts "*For Kids.*" Needless to say, I put it in my pocket for future reference.

Waiting for the hospital to get its act in gear is almost more of an effort than getting Bruce there. I twice in forty-five minutes have to angrily insist on getting the foot-tapping Bruce some sedatives. The head nurse on duty holds up her hand both times and waves me off. "They are looking for the drugs," she says distractedly.

I decide to get some airtime and call the head office to impress upon them to give Eve and Bruce some of their money back. Godfrey hands me several airtime tickets of very little value. It might take me a year to dial them all in.

I sit down next to a dozing Bruce. *Boop! Boop! Boop! Boop! Boop! Boop!* I press the digits into the phone. *Boop! Boop! Boop! Boop! Boop*! I don't see Bruce look evilly over at me from the corner of his eye as I push in more digits. *Boop! Boop! Boop! Boop! Boop!*—

"THAT'S F—KING IT!" Bruce roars and jumps from his seat. He kicks their bags completely across the reception room. "Give me that GODDAMN PHONE!" He steps toward me with his eyes blazing, his hand out. I turn slightly away from him and cover the phone. I look him in the eye and calmly say, "No, Bruce. It's my phone. Get your own." I can't say why I am so calm about it. I should be racing down the hall.

He jumps over to their bags and starts ripping them open. I walk a few steps to the nurse's station and interrupt an interview of a patient there. I am beyond caring. "I'm sorry, ma'am, but this man I told you about," I step from the doorway so she can see Bruce behind me well on his way to destroying the reception room, "is going to destroy your hospital one brick at a time. It's not my problem anymore. I suggest you find the people who are finding those sedatives." She bolts past me and down the hall.

I stand in front of the exit doors so Bruce cannot leave. Eve cleverly tells Bruce to look in all the nooks and crannies of their bags. He is ferociously rummaging through their stuff when a twenty-something, red-headed doctor from the United States walks in, trailed by a tall, bearded, hippie-looking nurse from Canada. "Bruce?" he queries to us.

Bruce jumps up from the bags. "Who are you and where the f–k is my phone?" Bruce rages. The doctor, totally unperturbed, says, "I'm Doctor Redhead, and this is my assistant, Nurse Hippie. I don't know where your phone is. May we take a look at you, Bruce? It seems you have some wounds to take care of."

Bruce waves him away. "I need to find that phone, now!"

I wave the doctor over as Nurse Hippie watches Bruce closely. We introduce ourselves, and I explain the situation. Dr. Redhead nods, absorbing the much-shortened version of the Lariam days spent with Bruce.

"I'm sorry we couldn't find the drugs sooner, but this hospital, although new, doesn't have a psychiatric ward yet. They don't have anything appropriate for Bruce's situation," he explains.

He can see the despair in my face. "Don't worry. We are going to administer him some drugs used to put people out for surgery. Will he take a needle?"

I have no idea, but I'll *definitely* take one.

Dr. Redhead consults with Nurse Hippie, and they come up with a game plan. Dr. Redhead calls, "I'll be back!" and strides quickly down the corridor. Nurse Hippie comes over to me and walks me through the reception doors.

"Had quite a day, huh?" he asks good-naturedly.

"You have nooooooo idea, my man!" I quip.

He laughs. "Actually, I have a good idea. I've gone loopy on Lariam myself. *Horrible* stuff! I can't believe they still prescribe it anywhere." I agree one hundred percent. "This is what we're going to do," he suggests. "We'll tell him the needle is an antibiotic for his cuts and scrapes. It will be the knockout drug. Later, after he is out, we'll take care of the wounds with an actual antibiotic." *Sounds good to me.*

We go back into the reception room and find Bruce with Eve's phone in his hand. He curses and shakes it. She looks very nervous as it is her only line to outside Africa. I hold up a hand to tell her that it is going to be alright. She holds up her hand to show me the phone battery in it. *Clever girl.* No phone calls to the Philippines from this reception room.

Dr. Redhead reappears from down the hallway. "The room is ready for you, Bruce," he says calmly.

Bruce glares at him. "I don't need a room. I need phone reception!"

"I understand, Bruce, but first we need to take care of those wounds on your hands and knees. If we don't clean them, you can get infected."

Bruce looks down at his hands and knees. They look bad even to an absolute madman. "Yeah, I guess," Bruce agrees.

"Come on. Right down here." The doctor waves for Bruce to follow him. We all do.

Three tranquilizers, two antibiotics, four temper tantrums, several leather limb straps, and an hour later, Bruce is snoring peacefully in the hospital bed, Eve's phone still clutched in his hand. Dr. Redhead comes out to where Eve, Ann, and I sit on a bench. "Let me take a look at your wounds," he says to me. I had completely forgotten about me.

"Is this blood on your shirt your's or his?" he asks.

"Mostly his," I retort. Except for a scratch along my ribs, a bloodied elbow, a bruised head, and two throbbing ears, I feel, well, *swell*. The doctor kindly cleans my scratches as he gives us the good and bad news. Well, the bad news, anyway.

"It could take him awhile to snap out of this. At best, in a few days. At worst, well, there are some people who never recover. We'll have to wait and see. This hospital doesn't have the facilities to handle him. I don't know if there is a hospital in Arusha that can. He most likely will have to go to Nairobi, but he can't travel awake if he is psychotic," the doctor explains. Eve appears crestfallen, and I can't blame her at all. We are leaving the following day, and she will have to deal with her father by herself.

"Is there a place where Eve can stay while you tend to him?" I ask.

"I'm sure the nurses can set up a room for her," Dr. Redhead offers. Nurse Hippie goes off to find the nurses to make up a room for Eve. "Let me know if you have any more questions," Dr. Redhead says and strides away to finish his rounds.

"Doc?" I call to him. He stops and I run up to him. "When he awakens from the psychosis, will he remember any of this?"

"The truth is," he responds, "many don't remember anything. They are unable to recall any event they experienced during the psychosis. It's probably the only upside to the whole thing."

I sure as hell hope Bruce doesn't remember. I know Eve will never be able to forget this.

I stride back to Eve. "Are you going to be alright, Eve? Do you want to stay with Ma back at Meserani? She'll take good care of you," I promise her.

"No, Mat," she says bravely. "You've done more than enough. Way more than enough. I'll call my mom and the insurance company in the morning and figure out what we need to do."

I give her my and the office's numbers. "You call me or ATC if you need anything, okay?"

She wipes a tear from her eye and hugs Ann. "Thank you *so* much for everything, Ann. Dad couldn't have made it here without you. Without you *both!*"

"Or *you*," I add. "You have been so brave, Eve. Please remember this person is not your dad. He's a good man beyond the Lariam. I hope he awakens himself as soon as possible." She nods and wipes away more tears.

I can't help but feel we are leaving people behind enemy lines. My only consolation is that the Big Boss returned their money to them and offered them a return trip any time they wanted. I don't imagine that will be anytime soon.

On the way back to Meserani from the hospital, there is a tired silence. I say to Ann, "I can't believe how calm you were during this whole debacle. I kid you not when I say you are one of my heroes. You were *amazing.*"

She waves it off. "It was nothing for me, really. I've had plenty of experience with psychotics. Let's face it. He thought I was his mother! He was never going to hurt me, even though I had three security breaches near the end there!" she chuckles.

"I got you beat, Ann. I had five!" We laugh together knowing we will never forget this.

As we pull up to Meserani at 11:30 p.m., six hours after we had left in the taxi, a question occurs to me. "You know when Bruce was on top of me and I had him locked up for a moment?"

She nods. "I told you psychotics had immense strength," she says with a smile.

"You weren't lying, but it felt like a crane had yanked him off me. Was that the Tanzanians?" I query.

Ann laughs and claps her hands. "Ha! Ha! No, not them! That was me! I did! I came up behind him and tried kicking him in the testicles. When that didn't work, I grabbed him by the belt and just pulled. I couldn't believe how easy it was!"

I laugh hard at that. I wouldn't have thought it possible for me to have an even greater admiration for her, but I do. "Well, seems like you saved my life as well. I guess I'm going to have to buy you a beer, Ann."

She smiles back at me. "I'll take it, Mat. I'll take it."

POSTSCRIPT

The next few days we hear nothing from Eve. What little we do hear, we get from the office. Apparently Eve's phone is never again quite right. Eve and Bruce spend six days in the hospital in Arusha. Bruce still does not recover from his psychosis. They then travel to Nairobi, where Bruce remains in a psychotic state for another five days.

On the twelfth day, Bruce comes out of his psychosis, and the exchange between daughter and father goes something like this:

"Where are we, Eve?" Bruce asks as he awakens.

Eve can see her father is back. "We're in a hospital in Nairobi, Dad. You had a psychotic episode from the Lariam you were taking for malaria prevention."

He doesn't believe her. He doesn't remember anything. "Nonsense! We need to get back on the truck immediately and continue our trip together," he states emphatically.

"That, Dad," Eve sighs, "will have to be planned for another time."

CHAPTER FIVE

ELEPHANT MEMORIES

PEANUTS FOR ELEPHANTS?

"Peanuts? Hmm," I say as I lay the snack goodies on the tablecloth next to our roofless Land Rover. It is customary to treat the guests to Sundowners halfway through the afternoon game drive. Sundowners consist of wine, beer, sodas, and assorted snacks like biltong (beef or antelope jerky), dried fruit, potato chips, and dried boerewors (beef sausage). This afternoon we have stopped for our peanut-accompanied Sundowners where we can watch the elephant herd graze lazily on the western hills a good eight hundred yards away. This is the first time in my six months of guiding at my lodge that we've had peanuts. I love peanuts. So does somebody else, seemingly.

"Elephant!" yells Vern, my twenty-one-year-old sidekick, a trainee at Leeuwenbosch Lodge. I turn around from fishing another beer out of the cooler box for Arnold, one of our four, fifty-something guests from England. My eyes widen and I smile. It is Norman, our dominant bull elephant and one of the stars of the reserve.

He is directly east, about four hundred yards out, and heading toward us through a thicket. Strangely, his massive ears are splayed and his trunk pointed straight out in front of him. It is as if an invisible rope was attached to the trunk's end and we were pulling on it. It is something I have never seen him do previously. It is something

I've never seen *any* elephant do. The couples look and an audible gasp escapes their lips. Even from here, Norman is impressive.

"Everybody on the vehicle!" I advise hastily. "You may take your drinks with you. I'm sure he's heading for the herd on the hill." It occurs to me to be safe, just in case the old wives' tale that elephants love peanuts is true. Obviously, peanuts are not something elephants find in the wild. Therefore, the possibility Norman is coming for them seems ludicrous. However, it is better to be safe than have your peanuts stolen by a bull elephant.

As Vern helps the couples onto the Landie and I pack everything into the cooler, I contemplate our great fortune this afternoon already. It has been phenomenal: we have seen three white rhinos; giraffe; our melanistic (black) springbok; a Uroplectes scorpion; our herd of buffalo with its new one-week-old calf; our herd of eland; two herds of our reserve's rarest antelope (Oryx and Waterbuck); the cheetah and her new, two-month old cubs (something one *very rarely* sees unless someone with telemetry has found her); an Addo Flightless Dung Beetle, which is even rarer; and a granulated, thick-tailed scorpion, one of Africa's most venomous animals. Having Norman come by to say hello would be yet another treat. I look behind me as I swing the packed cooler into the back of the Landie. I nearly drop it.

As I turned to pack away our goods, Norman must have started chucking it. He is now only two hundred yards away and on a mission. What is most disconcerting is that, even from here, I can see the fluid weeping from his temporal glands, which indicates he is back in *musth*, a period when testosterone levels soar, which can occur in bull elephants up to seven months of the year. It signifies his I-want-to-breed, woe-to-he-who-impedes-me mode. I slam the back gate and scuttle into the Landie.

Kneeling in the driver's seat looking backward, I confront the three concerned and one terrified face in front of me with what I hope is a reassuring smile. "Don't worry, all. Norman is an Addo bull from Addo Elephant Park just down the road. Addo elephants are arguably the nicest wild elephants in the world. The public wouldn't be allowed to drive themselves in the park if they weren't."

I don't mention the last time I saw Norman in full musth (when the bull also drips testosterone-rich urine from his penile sheath, giving him what is known as "green-leg") when he chased a small herd of mortified kudu (beautiful, spiral-horned antelope) and then turned on my vehicle. Trumpeting like the End of Days, he chased us for fifty yards down the road before I decided to drop gear and leave him and his testosterone safely behind.

Due to lack of time, I also fail to explain to them that animals tend to respect, for the most part, the right to first arrival in a location—there first and, thus, not a threat if not a recognized predator. Dominant animals, like elephants and rhinos, also tend to respect other creatures (like Land Rovers and their passengers) that do not move away. The psychology of it is simple: they are accustomed to most animals departing with great haste when they make their presence known.

If a creature refuses to leave when the usually dominant animal arrives, it means the refuser may very well be a more dominant animal. It is the main reason one should never run from an animal. Even a useless blob of human flesh remaining stationary may bluff a seven-ton elephant into believing that the human can whup his enormous butt if provoked.

"Sometimes Norman likes to buzz the vehicles when he's in musth, or heat, as you might say, just to make a display of his dominance ," I tell them. "If he comes over to us, please just stay very still and very quiet. No photos, please. It'll be just fine."

Beyond their shoulders, Norman, his trunk still pointed directly at us, with his ears open, pushes himself through the thicket that lines the small clearing where we're parked, seventy yards away.

Nancy, Arnold's wife, a woman who professed upon arrival at the lodge, "I do not want to do this safari thing. I'm *terrified!*" looks just that: terrified. She is just this side of reason and sanity. I realize I need to appeal to that last vestige of reasonability.

I look her in her eyes and say calmly, "Nancy, move to the middle of the seat… There you go… Now, just put your head down and close your eyes. I promise you, it is going to be fine. Norman may just come by to say hi, but he won't hurt us. We are going to be fine…Go ahead." I look at the others watching Norman. They are nervous but also excited. Allowing herself one last anxious glance, Nancy closes her eyes. She lays her head on her arms.

At thirty yards, Norman is exactly as he has been. *We,* not the herd, are unquestionably his first destination. There is *something* on the vehicle that he smells and wants. I can only assume it's the wine or beer they have in their hands now that the snacks and peanuts have been sealed away. "Everybody hand Vern your drinks," I say calmly but sternly.

They hurriedly pass their drinks forward. I nod at Vern to start throwing them over the side so I can watch Norman in case he decides to charge. Vern pours them over the side, one by one. He may as well be whistling "Dixie" in his nonchalance. *Rookies*.

Norman is sixty feet away and not stopping. I grab the rest of the drinks from them and Vern, and I fling them from the vehicle as far as I'm able—goblets, wine, and beer flying everywhere.

At thirty feet, I raise my left hand as far above my head as possible to make myself bigger and give Norman a signal of greeting. I start my usual monologue reserved for the elephants when they come this close to the vehicle. My voice is calm, soothing and, as it needs to be, absolutely assured : "Hi, Buddy! Nice to see you! You're looking good today, as usual…"

Norman stops at twelve feet and looks at me with his long-lashed left eye. He drops his trunk to the ground, and he turns his

head slightly to listen. "Just here having some snacks, my man…"
I babble. The two tips of his trunk explore the ground next to the
Landie. I can't help but think, *Sorry, Homeslice, no peanuts for you,*
and then I continue babbling: "On your way to visit the family? I'm
sure they'll be happy to see you. We're always happy to see you…"
Norman doesn't answer but continues to listen and search.

Towering over the vehicle, Norman is ENORMOUS. Twelve feet
at the shoulder and somewhere around seven tons, Norman at
thirty-five years is bigger than most elephants at fifty or sixty years.
(Elephants tend to grow their whole lives.) Even as I kneel in the
driver's seat, his eye is well above my head.

We hang here like this for ten seconds, the tip of his trunk
searching, searching, searching. It is a seeming eternity. He turns
his massive head toward us and takes a tentative step. The tips of
his tusks are now six feet from my face. He begins to slowly lift his
trunk. *Game over.*

"NORMAN!" I roar at him, shaking that very intimidating weapon
of destruction, my finger, for emphasis. "You KNOW better than this!"

He pulls his head back like I just smacked him. He leans his gar-
gantuan body away as if he's ashamed. "Keep going, Buddy! You just
keep RIGHT on goin'!" I bark again. He shifts, unsurely, and gives a
little head shake. Seeing I am still unfazed, he lumbers away dejectedly. I am as bewildered by his complete acquiescence as he is by my
failure to be impressed by him.

I turn back to the group when I see Norman is gone from us
for good. Three thrilled smiles greet me. There is no fourth smile.
Nancy's head is still down, her whole body quivering. She is going
to do just fine in this lifetime if she never sees another elephant or
safari vehicle. "He's gone, Nancy. You can sit up now," I tell her. She
does so reluctantly, her eyes darting left and right. If Norman were
still there, I'm pretty sure she would have died instantly.

Then the accolades pour in:

"That was amazing, Mat!"

"You're like…like an elephant whisperer or something!"

"He *totally* listened to you!"

I laugh and then explain the aforementioned concept of bluffing to them. They don't buy it. They much prefer the idea I am an elephant whisperer.

"What was he looking for?" Nancy asks.

"No idea," I answer honestly. "I have no idea. I've never seen him behave like that. As I've said, he's come by the vehicle for a buzz in the past, but the whole trunk-out-in-front thing is a new one for me. Good stuff, though, huh?" Nancy frowns. I can tell she wants to punch me in my peanuts.

The only thing I can think is different about today *is* the peanuts. I don't mention it, of course. The last thing I need is my guests running back to the lodge and their homes announcing that all elephants do have an empirical love of peanuts. That would be the end of my career as a credible guide. No matter how odd Norman's behavior was, it certainly wasn't empirical evidence that elephants, or Norman, like peanuts. On the other hand, maybe the mutual love of peanuts is why I have learned so well to be an "elephant whisperer." Only Norman knows.

JACQUES: A DAVID 2½ TIMES SMALLER THAN A GOLIATHS PENIS

We are camped at Thebe River Resort on the edge of the Chobe River in Kasane, Botswana. The resort is a delightful spot to rest in a four-star lodge or a tent when visiting one of Africa's premiere safari locations, Chobe National Park. As Thebe sits on the edge of the river, it is protected by an electric fence. The electrified fence is there for very good reasons.

The town of Kasane and, consequently, Thebe, are situated next to Chobe Park, a ten thousand, some-odd square mile area filled with Africa's most sought for animals and *the* place to see African elephants. There are no fences around Chobe and no fences around Kasane. The town sits unprotected between the park and the river. The river, especially during the dry season, is the animals' only source of water. Thus, one may find any number of these animals marching through town to get down to the river to drink, especially at night.

During the rainy season, the fence is turned off as the Chobe River overflows its banks and floods the closest third of the resort to the river. The flooding tends to cover not only the pool, the bar, and the biggest toilet block, but also the section of the fence closest to the river. This obviously raises a paradoxical problem. The fence cannot be left on, or the guests might be fried when stepping into any random puddle on the property. If the fence is disabled, however, Thebe's guests might have a midnight meeting with animals, particularly hippos, elephants, and buffalo, the ones most likely to have stomped down the unelectrified fence and entered the campsite.

Fortunately for Thebe, and for us, the camp uses other measures to protect against any possible marauding bandits or animals. These are, namely, guards, floodlights, and a secret weapon, Jacques. Jacques is a twelve-pound Jack Russell Terrier with the heart of lion and the feistiness of a caged honey badger. Jacques, categorically, does not agree with the idea that size matters. He proves this every day defending his home against the biggest and baddest of Africa.

From shooing fifteen-foot crocodiles from his doghouse during floods, to savagely biting the ankles of intruders in the dark of night, Jacques is uncompromising in his territoriality despite his diminutive size. He also has the pride of one who has become self-reliant in an annihilating world. If we try to pet him, he will cast us a side-long look of disdain and trot on by. If we offer him some of our lunch or dinner, he accepts it as an offering of homage for the service of keeping us safe while we're there. Somehow, as preposterous as it seems, we can't help but feel better for having him around, especially on the darkest nights…

Nick, our driver, and I are walking through the campsite after a long day of experiencing Chobe with our overlanding passengers. As Chobe is in flood, our campsite is well within the unflooded two-thirds of Thebe. With cloud cover, it is particularly dark this night. A branch snaps off to our left where the fence sits, so I stop and look through the trees in that direction. I'm hoping to see an elephant or two outside the fence. It is awesome to see them, their huge bulk dissolving into the darkness beyond the lights of the campsite. I have never seen an elephant on *this* side of the fence.

"Holy sh-t!" I exclaim as Nick joins me at my shoulder. "That's on *this* side of the fence!" We both stare at the bull elephant just to confirm it is not a hallucination. It is no more than sixty feet away. We are motionless for several moments.

"You'd better go tell the passengers, Rafiki," Nick says.

"That's an outstanding idea," I agree.

Nick and I run back to our campsite. A group of eight reluctant bed-goers sit chatting around the fire-pit. They look up at us, aware of our excitement. "What is it?" a passenger asks.

I can't help but smile broadly. "Anyone want to see an elephant *inside* the campsite?" They jump from their seats like hungry children invited to a candy store.

I go over some safety precautions before I take them over to a perfect viewing point hidden behind a line of small trees contiguous to a vacant campsite. It offers us cover and an escape route if the pachyderm is upset by our presence.

The elephant has moved to a spot twenty yards west of where he was before. He is a monstrous shadow in the dim light of the toilet block. He nonchalantly masticates an Acacia branch. I know he knows we are here. If he cares, he shows no sign of it.

We are ogling the pachyderm less than a minute before Jacques comes trotting up from the darkness behind us. His panting in our ears is almost painful in the silence between us and the bull. It is even louder for the elephant; he turns toward us and flaps open his ears, signaling his displeasure. Jacques muscles through the grass at our feet, the hair prickling on his neck. Napoleon, definitely on his own, has come to the front of the ranks.

There is a moment of tense silence. Jacques curls his lips back from his canines and growls. "Jacques, no!" I hiss and try to grab him. He bolts for the elephant, barking like a hound from hell.

I want to cover my eyes so I don't have to watch the bull stomping down on Jacques, turning him into a stick of furry gum on the bottom of his foot. It is impossible, however, not to watch the ferocious, miniscule David race up to the world's largest land-living Goliath, fearlessly voicing his rancor. The bull raises his trunk and trumpets down at the canine in anger and, amazingly, fear. Someone next to me yells, "Oh, *no!*"

Jacques races around the elephant's feet, barking with all of his twelve pounds. *Twelve versus twelve thousand*. The elephant tries valiantly to keep his eye on Jacques' comparatively microscopic, white form, but he cannot. The little yapping blur at his feet is a whirlwind of annoying noise and movement. What Jacques lacks in size he has in speed.

The elephant turns left. Jacques goes right. The elephant turns right. Jacques goes left. The elephant spins with an amazing agility, but Jacques stays behind him. It is too much for the elephant. With a final toss of his huge head and an ear-splitting trumpet, the bull turns on his tail and speeds away as fast as he can move his massive bulk.

As the elephant disappears into the darkness, Jacques stops just inside the light. He continues to bark like Cerberus at the gates of Hades. When the sound of the crashing elephant fades, Jacques, tiny and triumphant, trots proudly back to us. He stops before us and wags his stumpy little tail. We stare at him in silence, shocked to the core of our preconceptions of the logic of size in Nature. This dog, who weighs two and a half times less than that bull elephant's *penis*, has just frightened that elephant away. Who says size matters? Definitely not Jacques.

GEORGE:
PART I

Twilight's cool makes me shudder on the tracker seat of the jam-packed Land Rover. I look down at my feet hanging over the headlight, and a feeling of depressing unreality overwhelms me. I am a week into my safari-guiding education, and I am exhausted. We have been on a relentless schedule that I know I will not be able to sustain for the next few days, let alone a year.

We have been studying grasses all day, and I am flummoxed by them. There are around 9,600 different species of grasses in the world. South Africa boasts 10 percent of those species. I feel like we have studied all of them in the twelve hours I've been awake, and I still can't distinguish one from any other. With six months of this, with this much information, and this many hours a day, I'm pretty sure I will die long before I pass the Field Guides Association of Southern Africa's (FGASA) Level One.

I think of what I gave up to be here: most of my savings, my car, my condo, a directorship at a tennis club that paid me very well, and my family and friends. The only thing certain in my life at this point is that my future is uncertain *at best*. There is no guarantee that I will have a job at the end of the program, or that I'll even finish it.

I am actually starting to terrify myself with my thoughts when someone behind me yells, "Elephant!" Pieter, our professor and founder of our school, slows the vehicle to a stop. I raise my head up from my gloomy rumination to see the mammoth form silhouetted against the crepuscular sky, fifty yards down the road. It is George, the second largest, twenty-five-year-old bull elephant on this reserve.

George was one of the first "characters" I met a week before when I had first arrived on Amakhala Game Reserve. I was hobnobbing with my fellow students in Ulovane's main lodge when Pieter appeared. For some reason, he looked like a thirty-three-year-old, tough-guy version of a wisdom-filled rabbi to me. He looked us over with his studious eyes and asked us sans greeting, "Anyone want to see an elephant?" The five of us jumped up from the table and headed to this same Land Rover.

Pieter gave us George's background as we drove down Ulovane's driveway. "He is an Addo bull from Addo Elephant Park down the road from us. Addo elephants are, perhaps, the nicest elephants in Africa as they inhabit a park where a completely uneducated public can drive a car through the park and its elephant herds. With most elephants, one would never be this relaxed."

He told us that George, although very "nice" as far as elephants were concerned, was a bit of a worry. If anyone mistakenly left the electrified front gate open, George would take advantage of this opportunity and come into the confines of the school's encampment. As we rounded a bend in the driveway, we saw George thirty yards out from the front gate, decimating a small tree.

He was eyeing us as we approached the gate. Pieter hopped out and opened the gate and, as soon as the gate was open, George headed right for us. Pieter jumped into the Land Rover as he didn't have time to shut the gate again. He cleverly pulled the Land Rover forward to block George's cheeky advance through the gate.

George strode right up to the side of the vehicle, not five yards from our open-mouthed faces. He seemed to smile at us like he recognized the game we were playing. He took another step toward the space between the vehicle and fence post. Pieter cleared his throat and George stopped. Pieter looked at each of us gravely. "Although we call him 'George,' you must always remember that he, like all the other elephants on the reserve, is a wild animal. Don't ever mistake these animals for domesticated ones. Familiarity kills."

Looking at George standing there, rocking back and forth and "smiling" at us, it was hard to see him as a terrifying, death-dealing monster. He looked...well, *friendly*.

Pieter explained that if George really wanted to get by us, he could easily flip us over with his trunk, which houses over forty thousand muscles. After a few minutes, George realized that we weren't going to let him by. He didn't flip us over with his trunk. Without any complaint, he shuffled away to find easier browsing. I was filled with awe and knew immediately that I was going to love elephants—and this place.

This memory lightens my inner darkness momentarily. I look over at George for some more inspiration. He's busy pulling huge swathes of grass up from the side of the road. He cleverly whacks the long strands against his leg to rid the roots of unpalatable clumps of dirt. I can't help but feel there is something magical about him. I stare hard at George and think, *If you come over here, George, this will all be worth it. Even if I'm worn down to death over the course of this year, if you come over here right now, it will all be worth it. Please come. Please come.* Please *come.*

Not ten seconds pass when George looks up from the grass. He turns his huge head and looks in our direction. Unbelievably, he strides down into the road toward us.

It is the first time I hear, or rather, don't hear, the eerie silence of an elephant walking. In the soft dirt of the road, his "padded" feet make no noise as he approaches. Slowly, as if he is mesmerized by my wish, George draws inexorably closer. Forty yards, thirty, twenty yards, George looms larger and larger in front of me. It occurs to me then that I am the epitome of vulnerable on the front of this vehicle. I realize just as quickly, I don't care.

At fifteen yards, George emits a sound that is the most beautiful sound I have ever heard. It is a deep, sonorous rumble. I imagine it is the sound Earth would make (if it were to make a sound) rotating on its axis. It is known to hunters as a "stomach rumble." Actually coming from George's nasal cavity, it is an elephant contact call. *George is trying to make contact with us.* It rolls through me like thunder. I draw in an audible breath.

Pieter catches my reaction and whispers loudly, "Mat, don't move."

I'm not going anywhere. George rises up before me at five yards, his eyes easily four feet above my head. It is my turn to be mesmerized. His scent, his bulk, his presence in front of me is the whole world. He is a giant, blood-pumping planet. He *is* the entire universe. I stare up at him before me, frozen not in fear, but in absolute wonder. I have to fight with all my will not to reach up and touch him.

I can't say how long we hang there like that. It is as if he is waiting for an answer to his elephant salutation. Having "heeded" my telepathic pleading and having answered with his contact call, George is met with nothing more than our awe-inspired silence. He rocks his head slightly and tentatively lifts his trunk. It is enough for Pieter. "Mat, I'm going to roll back." Pieter steps on the clutch and the Land Rover rolls gently back from George. I feel like an invisible umbilical cord has been snapped between us.

George lifts his head back as if our departure is an affront. He has made contact and now we have moved away from him. I want to get down off the vehicle, approach him, and re-establish our seeming momentary connection. George turns side-long to us. He takes two steps and drops an enormous, steaming pile of dung on the road. He follows up that performance with an endless stream of urine. After his deluge, George wanders off into the coming darkness. When I turn and look at the eleven people behind me, most wide-eyed with fear , I see that they thought I would be turned into strawberry jam. "That was *AWESOME!*" is my response.

We drive the short trip back to Ulovane in the darkness. Alone again with my thoughts, I marvel that I have gone, in the span of five minutes, from perhaps the lowest moment of my life to the greatest. I quiver once again, but it is not the crepuscular chill that makes me shake; it's that I have just been privileged with the *best moment of my life*.

GEORGE:
PART II

It is my birthday. I have been at Ulovane for a month and have fallen into the rigor and structure of our days. I have been fueled time and again not only by seeing George on the reserve, but also by discovering all the animals that make up the ecosystems of Amakhala. I have figured out the grasses. I have even learned to love them (if such a thing is possible) by understanding that we humans, as well as most of Earth's herbivores, would not exist if it weren't for grasses.

I sit at the table of the lodge, studying. Pieter, Colin (thirty), and Trish (twenty-six), Colin's wife, have proven to be exceptional guide instructors. They want us to understand everything about everything. What they don't teach us themselves they tell us to research in our piles of books. One such pile is stacked in front of me.

Janet, twenty-five, an energetic, bright, and talkative Englishwoman and one of the four students in our year-long program, sits across from me. She's bored with studying and sighs, signaling a chat might be in order. I ignore her. She will prove to be our valedictorian, and I already recognize I do not have her retention abilities. Seeing I'm not biting, she gets up from the table and saunters over to the doors leading to the patio overlooking the reserve.

When she hisses at me, I think it is a ploy to start a conversation. I look deeper into my book. She hisses again with greater urgency. I flick my eyes to her and register the shock on her face. She zealously waves me over. I shake my head, "What?" She glares at me, tucks her arm against her, and with short, vicious jabs of her finger, points to something obviously worth seeing to the left of the door. She mouths, "*George!*".

I jump up from the table and race to the door expecting to see George near the patio. I nearly fall over her when I see George *is* the patio. Eating from a Common Guarrie tree overhanging the patio, George is no more than three yards from us. My bumbling presence at the doorway startles him. He backs from the patio, taking the huge branch in his mouth with him. *George, 1. Guarrie, 0*. He strides away, keeping a watchful eye on us.

We watch him go around the porch to Ulovane's fence-line. We can see he intends to feed off the trees just inside the camp. As he goes, he makes sure not to touch the yard-and-a-half-tall fence that harbors nine thousand volts of electricity. Janet and I race to the tents to let the other students know that George is gracing us with his more-than-welcome presence.

We follow George along the fence. Another student, John, nineteen, joins us. George allows us to get within less than ten yards of him. We obviously know he knows we are there. Pieter's words that George is a wild animal still rings in my ears as we watch him. We sense absolutely no agitation from him whatsoever. I think he likes us being there.

For fifteen minutes we snap a number of photos of George plundering Ulovane's trees. It is the best birthday present I could hope for. After those fifteen minutes and a great deal of torn down branches (thankfully none of which falls and crushes the fence and thus shorting it), George backtracks around a dense cluster of trees toward Janet's tent. Janet, John, and I follow, hoping to get a photo of him in the clearing beyond her tent.

We get there just in time to see George poke his massive head through the trees. He is no more than twenty yards out from Janet's raised patio. Janet begins a diatribe in her pronounced English accent, one you'd expect to hear from the Queen to her dog: "Hello, George! You look so good today! It's so good to see you, George! You're such a wonderful elephant! Oh, it's so lovely to see you!" George turns toward us and opens his huge ears. Witnessing his reaction to Janet fills me with an indescribable joy yet again. I am amazed that this incredible animal would pay attention to *us*, members of a species that has decimated his own and, in most of Africa, relegated them to fenced-in reserves.

Janet keeps up the gooey diatribe, and George is enthralled by it. He takes a tentative step toward us. He takes another and another. Once again it is as if he senses our wonder. He strides to ten yards. By now, there is no question that George is going to come all the way up to us. I want it to happen more than anything, but Pieter's voice rings in my head: "Familiarity kills."

A stab of fear rockets through me. George can easily reach over the fence and grab us with his trunk if he so desires. I shush Janet with more vigor than I intend to, and she registers this immediately and stops. "Let's go in the tent!" I say. They clamber into Janet's open tent. I turn to follow, but stop. George has stopped as well. I consider him, and him, me. He rocks forward as if to continue his advance. I turn from him again and move toward the tent. Before entering, I look back over my shoulder to see George lifting his head back in the same way he had a month earlier. It looks like we've hurt his feelings.

A stab of regret shoots through me. He backs up from us to about fifteen yards and lets out a small rumble. Not knowing what else to do, I lift my camera and take another couple photos. I don't want him to leave. Without any response from us, George lumbers away. A sudden sadness grips me. I can't help but think he was trying to bridge the gap between us. No matter what I feel, I try to console myself with Pieter's admonition, "George is still a wild animal..."

GEORGE:
PART III

Drake and I are studying late into the night. It is close to eleven, and we have a lot more to shovel into our tired brains. We have another Ulovane test coming up and, again, we feel like we know a smidgeon of the mountain of information the test will cover. We hunch over our books under our desk-lamps, trying not to pay attention to the fans blowing warm summer air around the tent.

The fans and lights sputter and falter. We expect a short. I grind my teeth. "What the fu—?" I say and look over at Drake. Ulovane, being out in the middle of the reserve and built within the last couple years, still has some wrinkles in its systems. Usually we laugh about the water running dry, or the electricity failing, but tonight we want to get our studying in. "Not tonight," I utter. The lights flicker crazily and fans cough more strongly, like a scene from a disaster movie. I half expect our tent walls to start shaking. Drake and I look at one another and laugh nervously.

It continues for two full minutes. The lights and fans cannot decide to be on or off, and they seem angry about it. We sit back in our chairs and wait as the schizophrenic electricity bounces shadows everywhere. Then, as suddenly as it begins, it stops. All is okay again in the world it seems. Drake and I consider each other. "Looks like Ulovane strikes again," I say. We laugh and look back at our books.

A half hour passes before I turn off my light. I fall into a dreamless slumber. I have no idea of the heart-breaking nightmare that tomorrow holds for me.

It is 6:30 a.m., and we have already been walking for the better part of an hour. Colin, shouldering a rifle, leads us with his long-legged strides to a vantage point over Listern's fields. These fields, once tilled by old Listern before his farmland became a game reserve, glisten in the morning sunlight. It is a perfect day to be out on the reserve.

An overwhelmingly pungent odor on my hand is making it difficult for me to get the most out of the gorgeous morning. I have learned the hard way that one shouldn't leave one's hands to feel the thick grasses through which one walks. Colin chuckles when I ask him what the smell on my hand is. "Congratulations, Mat," he chortles. "You have found yourself a brown hyena pasting!"

But I don't feel fortunate. I certainly don't smell fortunate.

"Hyenas walk over a grass frond and allow the stalk to slide through their anal gland, leaving not one, but two different territorial pastings. One for identification of the animal, and the other as demarcation of the time it passed there."

I'm pretty sure I got both.

We walk farther on, just above Striata Street, a road on the reserve dominated by a ground-level plant known as Aloe striata. I look under several rocks for possible creatures as Colin peers through his binoculars down at Listern's fields. "Hmmm" escapes his lips. We all come to attention. Colin is a veritable artist at spotting animals. We learn to pay attention to him on these occasions because, quite often, if we don't look when he says something, we end up missing it. We all look where Colin is looking but see nothing. *Like usual.*

"One of the utility poles is down," he says. We look but don't see a fallen pole. Instead we see the power lines sagging to the point where the pole should be. The trees obscure the view of the pole itself. Drake and I look at each other and smile. Now we know why the electricity was going bonkers the night before. We don't think anything more of it as Colin leads us away from our viewpoint.

Hours later we sit together at lunch. I am trying to keep my hyena-pasted hand away from my face as I eat. Pieter is talking to us about the afternoon activities when Colin comes in. He sits quietly down next to Pieter. Pieter stops what he is saying immediately. "I have some bad news," Colin says. "Remember the utility pole we saw this morning? Well, George knocked it over. He was scratching himself on the pole and snapped it. Since the next pole is way up on the hill above the river, the weight of the cables brought them down on top of him. He was electrocuted... *George is dead.*"

We sit in stunned silence. I look down, trying to comprehend what Colin has just said. *I am NOT going to cry*, I say to myself. *I am not going to cry.* Something in my heart starts constricting. My face burns. I feel light-headed. *I am not going to cry.* Nobody says a word for a full twenty seconds as everyone tries to digest the news.

Across the table, Janet lets out a barely audible sob and something explodes in my heart. The tears burst from my eyes. I shove back my chair and race from the lodge.

I am running nowhere I can see as the tears well and stream down my face. I am vaguely aware of the "no, no, no,..." falling from my lips. *The giver of my greatest moment is dead.* When I was sitting in the comfort of my tent complaining and laughing with Drake about the failing electricity, George was dying under the power of that same electricity. *Why had I turned away from him on my birthday?*

Why had I not let him come to us? Maybe all he wanted was to be with us in the same way we wanted to be with him? Why…why…WHY?

I can't stop crying even when the others come to check on me. I am a tough guy who isn't supposed to cry. I hold my hand up to them and avert my eyes. They leave me to my woe, not wanting to watch; perhaps it's the incarnation of the same sorrow they have in their hearts.

Later in the afternoon, Pieter decides to take us to see George. I am torn. I don't want to go but feel I must. I don't want the last image I have of him to be him lying there beneath the power lines. I don't want to see him bloated and already beginning to rot in the roasting summer sun. I also can't stand the idea of him lying there by himself. In the end, I climb into the Land Rover, silent and aching. No one bothers to speak to me or each other. *Nobody* wants to see George in death.

The heat is unbearable as I sit in the grass ten meters from George, crying. The other Ulovane students and several other representatives of Amakhala's lodges buzz around George's huge carcass. I can't help glancing at George's already bloated body, his tree-trunk legs sticking straight out from his body like he is a giant balloon ready to pop. I force myself to look at the angry black lines that crisscross the expanse of his gray back and an enormous gaping hole cut into George's hind quarters as if a great white shark had been feeding from him.

A lodge owner needed meat to feed his spotted hyenas who had been removed from the reserve proper to protect the antelope populations. Nothing is wasted in Africa. I just want to close my eyes and make this go away.

When most of the people are satisfied with their scrutinizing of his body and move off, I approach George. I can barely see him through my tears. I know I will never *not* cry when I think of these moments. I hear someone say that an autopsy would be an incredible thing to see on an elephant. Frederick, Amakhala's vet, says he doesn't think an autopsy would be a great idea. The cause of death is obvious, and an elephant dissection requires a chain saw and a bodysuit. I feel sick as I hear this. *Taking a chain saw to George.*

I stare at the hairs that jut from his leathery skin. "Mammal" is the word that pops into my head. *We are both mammals and have hair,* I think. I avoid looking at the huge, gaping hole on his haunch as I walk around his back end. A line of feces runs from his anus and onto the ground, forming a large pile there. There is no dignity in this death. I shift my eyes quickly to his tail. The hair hanging from the end of his tail looks like wire.

I tentatively reach out my hand. Touching him almost feels sacrilegious. *We weren't able to touch him in life; why should we be able to touch him in death?* I gently finger the wiry hairs on his tail. I run them through my fingers. Four come off in my hand. They feel fake, like plastic. Holding them, I realize I want to keep them, that I *must* keep them. I don't want George to ever disappear from me. I slide the hairs into my pocket and continue around his jutting leg.

I grit my teeth as I look at his massive, flaccid penis laying like a dead python beneath his swollen belly. The appendage that one day may have provided him with progeny that we, perhaps, could have lived side by side with for sixty years plus, has been rendered irrelevant. Red ants swarm over the tip of it, hastening George's disintegration. It is enough for me. Fingering the hairs in my pocket, I climb back into the Land Rover and wait for Pieter to drive us back to Ulovane.

Two weeks later, one of the herd females gives birth to a tiny calf. Everyone is ecstatic, not knowing that she was pregnant. It is Janet who voices what I am thinking upon hearing the news: "I am going to think of it as George's baby." There is enormous consolation in the thought, although I know it is highly unlikely that it is George's. As big as he was, he was still significantly smaller than Norman, our dominant bull. It is common knowledge that elephants will only breed with the dominant bull in a given area.

When I see the baby for the first time, I realize it doesn't matter if it is George's or not. Another baby elephant has been born on Amakhala. If our elephants are creating new generations, then all is not lost. Our connection to them will still be possible. George will live in every elephant I get the privilege to see while I guide in Africa.

One year later, after graduating from Ulovane, I return to Phoenix to visit my family and friends. I have George's hairs hidden away between the pages of my journal. I don't want to keep them there. I want them to be somewhere where they can be seen. I take two of the longest hairs and glue them to a canvas. They curve nearly parallel to one another, almost meeting at the bottom of the page. They form the head and trunk. A third hair I cut into two more pieces. The longest I curve across the page; it is a tusk. With the smaller piece, I make an ear. The eye is a small African porcupine quill found on Amakhala. The head on the canvas is an elephant. It is George.

The moment I finish it, I know who it will be for. I want it to be with someone I care about who may learn, one day, to love elephants the way I now do. I give it to my five-year-old goddaughter, Sophia. She has already insisted that for her tenth birthday, I take her to Africa. I know at this age she cannot understand what this gift to her means to me. Later, however, I am overjoyed by the fact that the African elephant has become her favorite animal.

"George" now sits on a mantelpiece in her home, occupying a place of honor by the dining room table.

ABOUT THE AUTHOR

Mat obtained his safari-guiding credentials from the Field Guide's Association of Southern Africa in 2007. He worked on Amakhala Game Reserve in South Africa as a guide for six months and then decided that he wanted to see more of Africa. In 2008, he joined one of Africa's premiere overlanding companies, Africa Travel Company. For nearly four years he worked with ATC as a guide in both East and Southern Africa until deciding to create his own company, TIA Safaris.

Mat now divides his time between the States and taking clients on the trips of their lives into the Africa he knows and loves. You can contact Mat through TIASafaris.com or its phone number 1-602-561-7823.

45064138R00120

Made in the USA
Lexington, KY
17 September 2015